PSYCHOFRAUD

AND ETHICAL THERAPY

JOHN DAVID GARCIA

WHITMORE PUBLISHING COMPANY

ARDMORE, PENNSYLVANIA

ISBN 0-87426-032-9
Library of Congress Catalog Card Number: 73-92028
Published by Whitmore Publishing Company, Inc.
35 Cricket Terrace, Ardmore, Pa. 19003
Manufactured in the United States of America

to

the victims of psychofraud

that they may find a better way

Contents

Preface

Having learned from experience that the usual trappings of success—sensual pleasure, riches, and fame—were not in themselves lasting sources of satisfaction, I resolved to find a way of achieving a truly meaningful life. I had long felt, without knowing why, that the greatest joys in life came from learning and helping others learn something that was true, new, and important. However, I saw the cleverest persons around me obsessed, not with knowledge, but with convincing others that they had knowledge. In so doing, it seemed to me, they deceived themselves and others about what was truly important. They seemed more concerned with being or appearing clever than with seeking truth. They usually strived to excel in a very narrow field which they never related to the rest of human activity. I asked myself, "Can a person be truly intelligent and creative while ignoring matters which affect the very survival of our species?" I decided that this could not be the case.

I had found that businessmen cared mainly about making money and that academicians cared mainly about proving how clever they were. Surely, I thought, those persons who have deliberately chosen careers in organizations that have no other stated purpose than to help people and to guide public policy must be wiser than the businessmen or the academicians. I therefore joined those persons who are politicians and/or work for government agencies and non-profit foundations to see if they were living worthwhile lives.

After having worked with them for a time, I found them as venal as the businessmen but much less courageous and as irrelevant as the academicians but much less clever. Furthermore, it seemed to me they were not really trying to help anyone except themselves by acquiring power or finding a secure, bureaucratic niche within a large, seemingly immortal organization. This left me in a quandary, for it seemed that there was no way one could lead a truly good and creative life and still be part of the rest of society.

I decided that what had to be done was to change society into something better. I considered the communist approach an utter failure, both in its orthodox and "new left" forms. I could not accept the mystical approach which was becoming increasingly popular. I chose instead an entirely new approach which involved a synthesis of evolution, science, and objective ethics. This approach was developed in considerable detail in my last book, *The Moral Society: A Rational Alternative to Death.*

Psychofraud and Ethical Therapy may serve as an introduction as well as a sequel to my last book. It is much simpler in structure and more limited in scope. My last book showed what has to be done from a social and political point of view. This book shows what has to be done from a personal point of view. My last book was about evolution on a cosmic scale. This book is about evolution on an individual scale. It is a book to help each person become more fully human and creative, while avoiding the lure of charlatans, false prophets, and others who prey on the gullible who are seeking truth and a more meaningful life.

The book should be read in sequence from the beginning. If the reader has forgotten some definitions or arguments, he can find them again with the help of the glossary or the index. However, the basic structure of the book is easy to follow.

Any errors in this book are solely my responsibility. I would like to thank my editors at Whitmore for their useful comments and suggestions. I would particularly like to thank Blair Simon and Tony Parrotto for their interest and help. I would also like to thank my friends Sandra Hass and Mary Ward for their extensive help in preparing the manuscript. Finally, I would like to thank the many readers of *The Moral Society* who have written to me, made criticisms, asked questions, and have been helpful in many ways. I hope that this will answer some of your questions.

John David Garcia

Potomac, Maryland
November 20, 1973

Introduction

"Grow or die" is a basic law of nature. Nothing stands still. Everything in the observable universe seems to be evolving or decaying. All known living organisms begin to decay physiologically once they stop growing. For human beings, there is an alternative to physical growth. Human beings can grow mentally all their lives. Furthermore, what they have learned need not die with their bodies, but can continue to exist in their creations and in the knowledge that they engender in others.

Although while we are still quite young our individual bodies may begin to decay irreversibly until we are dead, we can each experience every day of our lives the beauty of creating and of learning new things and teaching them to others. In this way we can grow throughout our lives, and our fellow men can continue to build upon our knowledge and our creations long after we are dead. This is one way in which persons can give meaning and purpose to their existence and achieve a sense of immortality. For this reason many persons are interested in liberating their minds from the shackles of anxiety and other destructive emotions as a means of increasing their creativity.

In an effort to be more creative, persons will undergo many experiences, such as formal education, mystical indoctrination, and psychotherapy. Each of these approaches—and many other alleged means of expanding creativity—have glowing testimonials written about them and disseminated by their adherents. Yet in observing the proselytizers of these various systems of belief, one often gets the impression that their enthusiasm involves a great deal of self-delusion. Their certitude in the efficacy of their methods is almost always subjective and not objectively substantiated. These criticisms apply particularly to the mystical and the psychotherapeutic approaches to mental well-being.

The essence of the mystical approach to truth is that ultimate reality is subjective, not objective. It is our inner conviction, our direct perception of the universe through "satori" or "sanctifying grace" which counts and not whether our alleged perceptions have any meaningful correspondence to the objective world. This approach to truth has held hundreds of millions of persons in thrall for thousands of years. Entire civilizations, such as those of India and Tibet, have been built on a mystical basis. Yet the nations which seem most capable of coping with reality have used another approach, the scientific method, which seems antithetical to mysticism. Science is not based on belief or subjective certainty, but on the proposition that all models of nature are to be held in doubt until experimentally demonstrated. And even then they are to be held only as relatively and tentatively true until a better model comes along. Therefore, if one accepts the scientific method and all its implications, one must reject the notions that there is such a thing as ultimate absolute truth and that we can ever reach it. There are only increasing degrees of truth. Between science and mysticism there is that peculiar creation of modern man called "psychotherapy."

Psychotherapy is not a single coherent ideology, but a multitude of sometimes contradictory beliefs and schools which in one way or another claim that they can predict and control human behavior—particularly aberrant, destructive behavior. Some forms of psychotherapy are extremely objective and appear to have a sound scientific basis, such as those which are derived from the behavioristic school. Other forms of psychotherapy are almost totally mystical, such as those derived from that amorphous mass of doctrine called "humanistic psychology." However, all forms of psychotherapy claim that they can improve human behavior. What constitutes "improvement" is not always clearly specified. From our perspective, we will consider improvement anything which increases human creativity.

We define creativity objectively as the ability to reorganize some aspects of the total environment—physical, biological and psychosocial—into new patterns which increase at least one person's ability to predict and control the total environment and do not necessarily decrease this ability for any other person. This is a rather complex concept which will be elaborated and clarified throughout the book. Some schools of psychotherapy, such as the behaviorists, may deny that they are concerned with creativity or perhaps even that such a thing exists. The behaviorists claim only that they can induce or remove behavioral symptoms which are desirable or undesirable, as the case may be. The humanistic psychologists, however, are in general most concerned with "creativity," even though they may not clearly specify what they mean by it. However, all psychotherapists claim to be able to improve health.

The position that will be taken in this book is that for a human being, health is indivisible from creativity and that a person's creativity is the best objective criterion for his health. Whatever increases creativity is good, and whatever decreases it is bad. From this perspective we will examine the scientific validity of the various schools of psychotherapy to see if their claims are justified. As in most complex fields of human endeavor, there will be no simple answers. We will see that each school of psychotherapy has some value, but that the vast majority of their claims are scientifically untenable and in many cases approach deliberate fraud.

"Psychofraud" is the term applied to all models of human behavior which have no scientific basis. The practitioners of psychofraud may be perfectly decent, well-intentioned persons who sincerely believe that they are helping others through their techniques. These may include witch doctors, ordained priests, and certified psychotherapists.

Many psychotherapists have a very humble view of their profession and admit that they do not really know what they are doing but that they are merely responding to the immediate needs of their patients by offering them a special kind of friendship. They serve as sounding boards and mirrors through which the patient can hopefully perceive himself in a more rational and realistic perspective. These psychotherapists are not practicing psychofraud, but Ethical Therapy.

Any perspective which is real is ethical. The basis of Ethical Therapy lies in the search for what is objectively real and true and not merely for what is subjectively satisfying. In Ethical Therapy, as it will be developed in this book, we present less a medical treatment than a special kind of education which helps each person acquire an ever-growing respect and desire for objective truth. It is an education which teaches each person to see himself in a cosmic, evolutionary perspective, wherein the increase of intelligence, i.e., the ability to predict and control the total environment, is the only common denominator in the evolutionary process. Creativity is a unique means by which the human species begins to get control and direct its own evolution. Ethics, intelligence, and creativity are different, interrelated facets of a single evolutionary process which must be understood if mental health and human progress are to survive.

The ethical component of man is as important in the overall picture as the intellectual. The essential feature in ethics is the value put on objective truth. It is this value which is shown to be absent in the traditional forms of psychotherapy, which are concerned primarily with emotional well-being. It is also absent in behaviorism, which, in spite of its objectivity, makes psychofraudulent claims about human potential and is concerned with predicting and controlling human behavior as an end in itself and not for any ethical purpose.

It will be shown that only an ethical person can be an Ethical Therapist and that an overwhelming number of the psychotherapists are objectively unethical. Still, there are many ethical persons who practice psychotherapy. It is only through them that psychofraud can be eliminated in their profession and that truly effective Ethical Therapy can begin. But the problem of the unethical therapists remains.

Psychofraud cannot be eliminated if its causes and its manifestations are not well understood. The victims of psychofraud are being deceived and exploited by an often unscrupulous group of practitioners. Ironically, the practitioners themselves are the worst victims of psychofraud. It is in an attempt to help ethical psychotherapists correct their errors and save all victims of psychofraud from self-delusion and exploitation that we expose the corruption of the psychotherapeutic community and present an ethical alternative to psychofraud. This is not intended to be an unanswerable refutation of psychofraud, but rather an engenderer of doubt, which will make all persons more critical and scientifically demanding of the psychotherapeutic process. Hopefully, readers will also learn to see psychotherapy from an ethical perspective by seeing examples of the patently unethical practice of psychofraud.

Through examples and case histories it will be shown that psychotherapists often injuriously deceive their patients, themselves, and others. Clearly, not all psychotherapists are deliberately deceitful. But because of the influence which psychotherapists can exert over individual human lives, any unethical psychotherapist is in a position to do enormous harm to innocent persons. Consider the following case.

Early in 1973 a prominent psychiatrist was arrested for the attempted murder of his wife. It was charged that as chief examining psychiatrist of the state parole board he had sought to bribe a prisoner with a parole in exchange for the assassination of his wife. Later in the investigation it was discovered that the psychiatrist himself had twice been committed to mental institutions as a psychotic. He was in fact much more mentally unstable and aberrant in his behavior than most of his patients.

From our point of view, the important issue is not whether the psychiatrist was guilty as charged, but rather how such an obviously unfit person could acquire such an important position—a position which put the life and liberty of thousands of human beings at the mercy of his whims. The question which immediately comes to mind is, Was this an isolated, freak occurrence, or is it part of a larger pattern?

The psychiatric community has by far the highest suicide rate of any occupational group. This is an objective fact which might be indicative of mental instability. According to Dr. Phyllis Chessler (24), the psychotherapeutic community as a whole is sicker than its patients. But far more disturbing is the subjective impression one often gets in dealing on a purely social or business level with many alleged psychotherapists that these are aberrant, seriously disturbed human beings who became psychotherapists in a desperate attempt to get help for themselves. Their current aberrant behavior is an indication that many psychotherapists cannot cure themselves. Therefore, why should we believe that they can help others?

A few years ago a prominent professor of clinical psychology from a major university was arrested for making indecent advances to a police vice squad officer who was being used as a decoy for entrapping homosexuals. The professor claimed that he was merely doing "research" on homosexual behavior and that he had no illegal intent. However, the evidence against him was such that he was convicted. It was easily proved that he was a habitual homosexual, although currently married and a father. However, he was treated with sympathy by his colleagues and merely asked to seek "professional help." He took "medical" leave for a year instead of being fired for "moral turpitude" from his teaching position. He was considered a leading expert in "rehabilitating" persons with aberrant sexual behavior in general and homosexuals in particular.

At issue here is neither whether homosexuality should be considered a disease nor the ethics of interfering with private voluntary behavior and entrapment. The issue is, Do psychotherapists know what they are doing? Do they really know how to treat aberrant behavior? Do they even know what aberrant behavior is?

In the January 19, 1973 issue of *Science,* Dr. D. L. Rosenhan, a professor of psychology and law at Stanford University, reports on an experiment in which he and seven other normal, healthy professional persons had themselves committed to various mental institutions under the pretext that they were hearing voices (116). Once committed, they behaved normally and rationally, answered all questions truthfully, disclaimed any further symptoms, and tried to convince the authorities that they were sane. Although they were hospitalized for as long as 52 days, none of the staffs at these institutions ever detected them as pseudopatients. Instead, they attempted to pump them full of drugs. A total of 2100 doses of drugs, including powerful tranquilizers, were administered to the pseudopatients during their hospitalization. The pseudopatients were all diagnosed and labeled for life as psychotics. Elaborate psychiatric theories were propounded to explain their normal behavior as being symptomatic of psychosis. Ironically, many of the real patients in these institutions correctly identified the pseudopatients as imposters who were in fact sane. Several patients thought that the pseudopatients were journalists after a story. Clearly, in these cases, certified insane patients were objectively better at making correct diagnoses of persons' psychological states than were the "sane" psychotherapists. As Dr. Rosenhan concludes, "It is clear that we cannot distinguish the sane from the insane in psychiatric hospitals." If psychotherapists cannot do *this,* what can they do?

Psychotherapists claim that they can help mentally disturbed persons become well. They have developed many elaborate "scientific" theories to explain aberrant behavior. These theories range from the almost universally accepted medical theory of the eighteenth and nineteenth centuries that insanity was due to excess masturbation, to the extremely influential theories of Freud which related aberrant behavior to "unconscious sexual needs," to the modern behaviorist school, which claims that all human behavior is a result of operant conditioning and can be modified in any way we wish, solely by conditioning. Every one of these theories has deeply influenced millions of human beings, often depriving persons of their freedom and sometimes of their sanity and their lives (152, 153). Theories similarly suspect are currently being used to explain and allegedly control every facet of human behavior, from simple neuroses and anxiety to educational inadequacies and entire sociopolitical processes, e.g., Marxism. These theories have only two things in common: (1) they lack a scientific foundation, however much they may protest their "objectivity"; and (2) they are psychofraud.

Psychofraud is a complex, destructive psychosocial phenomenon to which all human society is prone. What it is, how it occurs, where it is taking us, and how we can overcome it are questions which will be answered. It will also be shown that psychofraud is a process by which human beings corrupt their need to be more fully human, creative and ethical.

Ethics, as they will be discussed in this book, are not mystical, transcendental, existential, or mysterious. Rather, they are scientific, objectively derivable rules of how best to achieve our basic, innate goals. Psychotherapy and ethics are both concerned with human behavior. Psychotherapists often claim to be "value free." However, this is usually a specious claim, since almost all therapists distinguish between normal and abnormal behavior, and this is a value judgment. Although ultimate values cannot be logically derived from scientific facts, science can show what are the necessary consequences of pursuing one set of values versus another. It can also show us when our end goals are mutually exclusive and how we can best (in the mathematical sense of optimal) achieve all our logically self-consistent goals. It will be shown that our basic innate goals are all logically self-consistent. It is our acquired goals which are often self-contradicting. This is the basis of scientific ethics. This is the basis of Ethical Therapy.

Ethical Therapy is the counter to psychofraud. The contrast between Ethical Therapy and psychofraud is the subject of this book, which is a dynamic guide to help each reader fully develop what is best in him and achieve his full, human, creative potential. In so doing, we will direct a most severe criticism at those ideologies which purport to explain, predict and control human behavior in terms of psychofraud. These include some, not all, aspects of traditional religion, classical psychotherapy, behaviorism, humanistic psychology, neo-mysticism and many of the so-called social sciences. We attack all forms of psychofraud because there is no scientific evidence that the underlying assumptions in these ideologies have any validity in objective reality. Insofar as psychofraud works, it probably works through conditioning, suggestion, self-delusion and emotional catharsis to make persons "happy" but not objectively healthy or *more creative*. Psychofraud can create a fools' paradise, but it cannot contribute to human progress.

The self-delusions of psychofraud stem from the common human inability to live with uncertainty and self-doubt. Comforting illusions of certainty may make us happy for a while and bring us emotional well-being, but they do this at the price of diminishing our ethical intelligence. We share all of our emotions with subhuman animals. It is not our *emotions* which make us uniquely human; it is our *ethical intelligence*, which cannot grow in the absence of doubt. Therefore, the reader should approach this book in a spirit of skepticism. We will try to demolish the comforting illusions of psychofraud, but we will not replace them with new illusions. Instead, we will try to stimulate the reader to value ethical intelligence more than he values emotional well-being. If we succeed in this, then we will also succeed in helping the reader live with doubt. This is Ethical Therapy.

To understand Ethical Therapy is to doubt its validity. To use Ethical Therapy is to continuously demolish and recreate its theoretical basis. Ethical Therapy is based not on methods, but on goals. All the goals of Ethical Therapy are means for achieving the single basic goal of maximizing ethical intelligence.

The meaning and etiology of psychofraud are given in the first part of this book. The meaning and the rationale for Ethical Therapy are given in the second part. Together, both parts are intended to increase ethical intelligence through creative doubt.

In order to be clear and unambiguous, what follows is written in an assertive, positivistic style. The following list of key concepts is included to alert the reader to the importance of the precise interpretation of words which are vulnerable to ambiguity. A more complete glossary is included at the back of the book. Many case histories and examples are used to help the reader get the "human feel" for the problem and to illustrate specific points. However, every description, hypothesis, theory, and statement may be in error. If the reader can accept this statement and still be interested in reading what follows, then he has already begun to rid himself of psychofraud and to use Ethical Therapy.

Key Concepts

A complete glossary is included on page 205.

CERTAINTY A state of mind in which no doubt exists about some cause-and-effect relationships. It is unethical to be certain about anything except the existence of our own thoughts and perceptions, which are not cause-and-effect relationships. The need for certainty may be the fatal flaw in human nature.

CREATIVITY The ability to organize the total environment—physical, biological and psychosocial—into new patterns which increase the collective ability of all persons to predict and control their total environment. Creativity is a direct function of intelligence and ethics.

EDUCATION Any process which increases objective truth for any organism; i.e., any process which increases any organism's ability to predict and control by increasing or altering the information content of the organism.

EMOTION A preprogrammed pattern of behavior, which predisposes an organism to behave aggressively, fearfully, lovingly, or in some combination of these patterns. The basic emotions are inborn and instinctive but can be modified by learning. Feeling, sensitivity, affection and joy are not emotions.

ENVIRONMENT The total environment has three primary dimensions—the physical, biological and psychosocial. The physical includes all matter, natural laws and their interactions. The biological includes all living organisms. The psychosocial includes all the behavior of all living organisms.

ETHICAL THERAPY A process for increasing creative intelligence by increasing ethics. The immediate objective is to reorient the ethical perspective of the person so that he uses the criterion of what maximizes objective truth in making every decision and relating to other persons. This process also eliminates neuroses and emotional blockages to creative behavior.

ETHICS Rules of optimal behavior which simultaneously maximize our ability to achieve all logically consistent goals. It can be shown logically and scientifically that rules of behavior are optimal if and only if they satisfy the criterion of maximizing objective truth.

EVOLUTION A process which increases the intelligence in the universe. The only common denominator in the evolutionary process is the increasing ability of the biomass to predict and control its total environment. Man is the only species known which can predict and control its own intelligence. This manifests itself in all creative behavior and cultural evolution.

HEALTH The physical and mental condition conducive to predicting and controlling the total environment. Whatever diminishes our ability to predict and control the total environment diminishes our health. When this occurs through physiological change, such as a broken leg, then it is our physical health that is diminished. When this occurs through a change in the information content of our mind, then it is mental health that has been diminished, and we say that the person is neurotic. When it is a combination of deleterious physiological and information changes in the nervous system, the person may become psychotic. The best objective indicator of health is creativity.

IDEOLOGY Any process or system of beliefs which claims to be able to predict and control some or all aspects of the total environment without showing scientifically that this is in fact the case. Ideologies are based on faith and are emotionally defended against any scientific contradiction.

KNOWLEDGE Information which enables or increases the ability of an organism to predict and control its total environment; i.e., information which is true and increases intelligence and health. Knowledge cannot exist independently of intelligence. A book contains information. Only an intelligent organism has knowledge.

LOVE Refers to a type of behavior as well as to an emotion. As an emotion it is a preprogrammed state of mind which predisposes us to behave in such a way as to enhance the welfare of another even at the cost of our own welfare. When welfare is seen as synonymous with happiness, then love is perverse and unethical. When welfare is seen as synonymous with creative intelligence, then love is natural and ethical. Ethical love can exist without emotion, as when a person makes a deliberate rational choice to maximize objective truth as an end in itself and increases the creative intelligence of others as a necessary means toward this end. Emotional love can be ethical in the case of protective nurturing and maternal instincts. Emotional love is easy to pervert as in the case of sadomasochists and in the case of parents who sacrifice objective truth for the happiness of their children.

MIND The set of all our thoughts and perceptions. Insofar as thoughts and perceptions are predictable and controllable, the mind is conscious. Insofar as thoughts are unpredictable and uncontrollable, the mind is unconscious. We know with certainty only the existence of our own minds. We infer from the behavior of other organisms and our own behavior and minds that other organisms have minds similar to our own insofar as they behave similarly to us. From this inference we can develop a mind model of behavior which can be objectively shown to enable us to predict and control behavior. The mind model is analogous to the model of gravity. We cannot perceive directly the existence of gravity, but it is a model which enables us to predict and control.

MYSTICISM Any systematic attempt to obtain truth through direct insight independently of scientific evidence and processes. Mystical truth is always of subjective origin. When mystical insights are supported by scientific evidence, then the mystical truth has become objective. There is no conflict between mysticism and science so long as mystical insights are not held to represent a higher reality than objective truth. It is in the nature of mysticism that its adherents tend to substitute subjective truth for objective truth and in the process become practitioners of psychofraud. All the major religions and the traditional ethical and psychotherapeutic systems seem to have a mystical basis. Objective evolutionary ethics and Ethical Therapy have a strictly scientific basis.

NEUROSES Learned patterns of behavior which decrease a person's ability to predict and control his total environment. Uncontrollable emotionality is not necessarily neurotic unless it has been caused by some learned experience; e.g., persons who are filled with hate for some particular ethnic group are neurotic because it is necessary to learn to hate a whole ethnic group, and this behavior decreases creative intelligence. Because neurotic behavior is learned behavior, it is susceptible to modification by all types of psychofraud as well as Ethical Therapy.

PREDICT AND CONTROL Refers to the essential property of intelligent organisms by which events are foreseen and made to comply with the organism's needs and desires. The ability to predict cannot exist independently of the ability to control and vice-versa. Although man could predict astronomical events long before he could control them (as in the case of artificial satellites), he could not have predicted any astronomical events if he could not have controlled his observational procedures by controlling his own biological sensors (eyes, ears, etc.) and the creation of amplifiers of his sensors, such as clocks, calendars and telescopes. Any event which is controlled is by definition predicted. Therefore, control is a higher property of intelligence than prediction, although each property is essential to the other. See definitions of *Prediction* and of *Control*.

PSYCHOFRAUD An ideology about human behavior. Any model which purports to predict and control human behavior and cannot be scientifically verified is psychofraud. Examples of psychofraud are found in all religions, political ideologies, and forms of psychotherapy.

PSYCHOTHERAPY A process for replacing information which decreases a person's ability to predict and control his total environment with information which increases his ability to predict and control his total environment. Psychotherapy is a special type of education and does not necessarily include the use of drugs or surgery, although these techniques can also change behavior and possibly even increase creativity. The best criterion for the success of psychotherapy is an increase in the net creativity of the person. Most of the treatments called psychotherapy seem to consist mainly of psychofraud.

REALITY That which we can (1) predict and control or (2) know that we can neither predict nor control. Our thoughts and perceptions are always real, but the models we create about what causes our thoughts and perceptions are not. Only that which is true is real. Only models which enable us to predict and control are true.

SCIENCE (Scientific Method) A process for expanding objective truth. It is based on the notion that all models of cause-and-effect relationships are assumed to be probably false until proven true by controlled experiments. No model is ever assumed to be beyond doubt. It is assumed that every model of cause-and-effect relationships can always be improved.

TRUTH Refers only to working descriptions and models of events and their relationships. A model of cause-and-effect relationships is true only insofar as it enables us to predict and control. Truth is subjective insofar as we believe that we can predict and control. Truth is objective insofar as we actually do predict and control. Subjective truth or intuition is often the first step in developing objective truth, but until verified it may include many false insights and concepts. Psychofraud can engender subjective truth. Only science engenders objective truth.

Part One

PSYCHOFRAUD

1

Genesis

In 1954 an intelligent, pretty, seventeen-year-old French girl, living in Paris, had a severe schizophrenic breakdown. The girl, whom we shall call Collette,* had been an excellent student with an active social life. After the breakdown she became slovenly and uncommunicative. She lost interest in everything around her and could not even care for herself. Her divorced mother, who worked as an electrical draftsman, had her committed to a sanitarium, but Collette made little progress. Eventually electric shock therapy was used, and Collette became more responsive to the world around her. After a time, she was able to live at home again; but she was no longer the bright, active girl she had been. She practiced the same profession as her mother, but she had lost her sparkle. She had been a voracious reader before the breakdown, but now she hardly read at all. She had little interest in social activities and lived a dull day-to-day existence.

Collette continued to receive psychotherapeutic treatment

* Not her real name.

in France and later in the United States when she came to live with her mother, who had married a black American soldier. After living in the United States, Collette married a friend of her stepfather; he was also black. She had a child and continued to have psychotherapy, but her mental health was clearly deteriorating. Her husband left her after becoming a black militant. Collette was now having severe emotional problems and undergoing a schizophrenic withdrawal. She could no longer hold a job or care for her child. Her mother, who was now separated, took charge of the child and had Collette committed to an American sanitarium. In the sanitarium she got progressively worse; not even shock therapy seemed to work. One psychiatrist claimed that her problems stemmed from her interracial marriage and her husband's abandoning her. Another claimed that her problem came from being dominated by her mother. Collette's whole life had been, so he claimed, an attempt to emulate her mother even to the point of acquiring the same profession and marrying a black man as her mother had. He made a very convincing argument with what seemed to be a sound psychiatric foundation.

It was decided that the best treatment for Collette was to be kept apart from her mother and her child. She did not see them for a year, and all the time her condition became worse. The rapidly deteriorating health of her daughter caused the mother to take her from the sanitarium and to change psychiatrists once again; Collette had already undergone therapy with five different psychiatrists. However, she was now so wasted physically as well as mentally that she was subject to infectious diseases.

Her mother took her home. A nutritionist was called in. He gave Collette massive doses of vitamins and nutrients. In a few weeks she looked much better. However, much to everyone's surprise, Collette had also completely recovered from the schizophrenic symptoms which had been getting steadily worse for several years. She was recovered to the point where she was as active and alive as she had been at seventeen. She has since been well, exhibiting no schizophrenic symptoms for several years. It was found that Collette's mental problems had stemmed from an organic disorder which could be treated with large doses of vitamins. She had spent fifteen years, her entire youth, suffering and receiving useless psychotherapeutic treatment. She was a victim of psychofraud (175).

The history of psychofraud is as old as man. Tens of thousands of years ago, our ancestors had the witch doctor drill holes in their skulls to let the evil spirits out. This was psychofraud. In ancient Babylon, young girls were sold into temple prostitution in order that their parents and future clients could obtain the favor of the gods. This was psychofraud. In ancient Rome and until very recent times, psychotics were tortured with red-hot irons and whipped to drive the devils possessing them out of their bodies. This was psychofraud.

During the Middle Ages, pilgrims travelled all over Europe and the Holy Land to touch the bones of some alleged saint in the hope that this would cure them of diseases ranging from leprosy to gout, or perhaps win them some prize ranging from a maiden's hand to a kingdom. This was psychofraud. We can see the same phenomenon today at Lourdes. Millions of Moslems, Hindus, Catholics and Protestants have died fighting each other in the belief that theirs was the one true religion and that to die in its service was to be assured eternal happiness in heaven. This was psychofraud. It is still happening in India and in Ireland.

Tens of millions of persons were slaughtered by the Nazis because they were considered to be of an inferior race and had to make room for the one true master race, the Aryans. The wealth and intellect of Germany, one of the most creative nations in history, was wasted perhaps forever in order to achieve this end. This was psychofraud.

Millions of persons sit in orgone boxes, go to palm readers, astrologers, priests, witches, and psychotherapists so that they may find spiritual and emotional comfort, guidance, and understanding. This is psychofraud. *Why do they do it?*

Psychofraud is practiced because it works. Psychofraud can unite nations, cure blindness, induce or remove warts, bring happiness to one's friends and death to one's enemies. Above all, it can bring inner peace and contentment. It can do this because people need to believe. They will believe the most outrageous nonsense if it promises them something they value. Faith may not move mountains, but it can move persons, even to self-destruction—both physical and mental.

Because of the interaction of mind and body, belief can have profound physiological effects (73, 140). These effects are not always beneficial, and they may in fact be deleterious in the long run. Nonetheless, these beliefs persist, and their physical effects have been documented and can be demonstrated scientifically. *Psychofraud* is any method, device, or process which changes our behavior only because of our belief in it and not because of its intrinsic merit. Psychofraud is an ideology about human behavior. *Ideology* is any belief in cause-and-effect relationships which is not supported by scientific evidence. Psychofraud cannot work when there is no faith. The more faith both the practitioner and the recipient have in its effects, the more effective psychofraud will be. At worst, psychofraud is destructive or ineffective. At best, it is a placebo.

PLACEBOS

Placebo is Latin for "I will please." It has long been known in medicine that physiologically inert or nearly inert substances, such as chalk or sugar pills, can have profound physiological effects, if the persons who take these substances believe they will work. When these substances are administered medicinally, they are called *placebos.* In their excellent treatise on placebos, Kissel and Barraucand (73) give the following formal definition of a placebo.

> A therapeutic measure of no intrinsic efficacy or weak efficacy with no logical connection to the illness but effective through a psychological or psychophysiological mechanism, if the patient thinks he is receiving an active treatment.

We say that a treatment has a placebo effect if this effect can only be produced when a person knows that he has been treated; if the person is treated without knowing it, there is no observable effect.

The history of medicine is primarily a history of placebos and their effects. This ranges from the sympathetic magic of 20,000-year-old Cro-Magnon cave paintings to the 4,000-year-old Babylonian practice of concocting and administering certain medicines only in the full of the moon; to ancient Egyptian cure-alls made of lizard blood, frog semen and hippopotamus feces; to the Roman wearing of necklaces made of wolves' teeth in order to prevent all childhood diseases and convulsions; to the treatment of Pope Boniface VIII for nephritis and colitis with a gold papal seal applied to His Holiness's right buttock; to the practice of bleeding persons suffering from infectious diseases with leeches in order to remove the evil humors from the blood; to the twentieth century treatment of mental illness by free association, dream analysis, Oedipal regression, primal screams, marathon tickling, sexual intercourse with the therapist and other patients, and similar modern psychotherapeutic techniques (23, 65, 66, 132, 161). It is important to note that all these placebos work. Most of the patients treated become and/or remain well, and most claim to feel immediate benefits after the placebos are administered (73, 91, 146, 112). This is the way medicine first developed and is still being practiced in this century. However, the scientific method was introduced into medical research in the nineteenth century. This was when truly effective medicine began to replace placebos.

Placebos and Science

The scientific method in medicine has been applied for the most part to the development of drugs and physical treatments. The placebo effect was first recognized early in the nineteenth century. This discovery resulted in part from the tremendous success of Cagliostro and later Mesmer in using hypnotism to treat many kinds of diseases. Mesmer's "animal magnetism" was the rage of European salons. It was disparaged by the orthodox physicians, but anyone who saw a public demonstration of Mesmerism was soon convinced. Through hypnosis, Mesmer restored the use of sight or limbs to persons who had been blind or crippled for years. He and others were able to induce general anesthesia in patients so that major surgery could be performed without pain and the subsequent death from shock. It soon became clear that mere suggestion could have powerful effects (95).

Subsequently, increasing numbers of medical researchers began to use a placebo control for testing the effectiveness of experimental treatments. This involved dividing treated patients at random into at least three statistically matched groups. One group was given the experimental treatment, another was given a placebo and the third, called a "control," was left untreated. By comparing the results on the three groups, it could be determined how much effect each "treatment" had.

Early in the nineteenth century a British admiral learned through hearsay that lime juice, regularly administered, could prevent scurvy. He ordered one of the first scientific medical experiments performed. Three groups of sailors were treated respectively with lime juice, placebos, and providence. The effectiveness of the lime juice was clearly demonstrated.

British sailors became regular drinkers of lime juice and, as a consequence, acquired the name "Limey" while avoiding scurvy. Napoleon ordered a similar experiment for testing the effectiveness of vaccinations. In a similar way, modern drug therapy, from quinine for malaria to penicillin for syphilis, has been developed. In the area of surgery, the scientific approach has not been as vigorously applied; and many types of operations, such as tonsilectomies, lobotomies, and hysterectomies, continue to be performed without the scientific determination of their full benefits and liabilities. These are not, strictly speaking, placebos, since they may have deleterious effects. However, many types of surgical procedures, such as cancer operations, are fully documented by comparative, long-term follow-up studies; and they can be shown to be effective in reducing the morbidity and/or mortality of the treated patients.

The latest scientific technique for controlling the vagaries of placebo effects is the "double-blind placebo control experiment." In this type of experiment, neither the patients nor the experimenters know when a placebo is being used. In this way, the experimenter will not inadvertently treat his experimental groups differently than his control, thereby biasing his results.

The only area of modern medicine where there is almost no scientific investigation of the effectiveness of alternate treatments is in psychotherapy (38, 148). There have been some attempts to investigate psychotherapy scientifically (91), but with few exceptions, modern psychotherapy seems to consist entirely of administering placebos (183). In some cases psychotherapy may be equivalent to destructive surgery when it has an iatrogenic instead of curative effect. *Iatrogenic* refers to illness induced by improper medical treatment. In his book, *Trick or Treatment: How and When Psychotherapy Fails,* Dr. Richard B. Stuart (148) has given many examples of psychotherapeutic treatments which led to a worsening of symptoms for "treated" patient groups while the "untreated control" groups got as well or better than the "treated" group. He concludes that traditional psychotherapy is at best a waste of money and at worst a harmful experience in terms of objectively measured behavioral changes. Studies by Eysenek (38), Kissel and Barraucand (73), Meltzoff and Kornreich (91), Strupp and Bergin (147), and many others lead to the same conclusions, even when they are trying to prove the opposite.

The power of placebos in psychotherapy is illustrated by the following examples:

> A 26-year-old man, depressed, a failure in his work, is becoming more depressed and increasingly neurotic even after two years of psychotherapy. He completely changes his personality after being treated by placebos for four months. He becomes dynamic, aggressive and successful (73).

> A 30-year-old woman is filled with anxiety and sexual frustration. Her symptoms disappear when she is treated with placebos. Treatment is interrupted because of an infection which is treated with penicillin. Again she is sexually frustrated and anxious, and symptoms again disappear when she is treated anew with placebos (73).

Classical psychotherapy seems at best to be a placebo (183). As any victim of "black magic" can testify, placebos can have deleterious as well as beneficial effects: witch doctors have been known to kill and cure with their spells. Although some forms of psychotherapy may cause damage, the overwhelming evidence is that, intrinsically, they neither harm nor help (73, 183). They are inert, very expensive placebos.

The $20,000 Placebo

Expensive placebos, ranging from pearls dissolved in wine to powdered rhinoceros horn, all intended to produce an aphrodisiac effect, have been used for thousands of years and are still used today. However, no placebo has ever been quite so expensive nor so widely used as modern psychotherapy. The typical Freudian analysis takes about three hours a week and lasts three to five years and often much longer. At the typical $50 per hour rate, this "treatment" will cost $20,000 or more. Thousands of persons have paid for this placebo, and they have been victims of psychofraud. Did they get their money's worth?

If we regard psychofraud as a form of entertainment which makes people happy, then it may be worth the price. Strupp, Fox and Lessler (146) in their report, *Patients View Their Therapy*, did a survey of psychotherapy patients. Over 90 percent expressed satisfaction with their therapy. They felt that they were better persons for having undergone therapy. Not many forms of entertainment can make similar claims. But $20,000 does seem a high price to pay for self-delusion, since there is no evidence in terms of objectively measured behavior that psychotherapy patients are better off in the long run than people who do not receive this therapy (183).

THE NEED FOR MAGIC

In Tennessee Williams' play *A Streetcar Named Desire*, Blanche DuBois says, "I don't want reality. I want magic." With these words she speaks for a large segment of humanity. Reality is often so unbearable that persons delude themselves into believing that things are not as they are but as they would like them to be. This is psychofraud.

Human beings seem to be born with an innate need to predict and control their total environment. When some aspect of their environment is unpredictable, uncontrollable, threatening and unavoidable, they will often delude themselves into believing that they can predict and control through some magic formula. For this reason primitive men propitiated or coerced the gods to control weather, fertility, and disease. Modern science has shown us more effective ways of dealing with the physical and biological environment; consequently only a few persons still try to use magic and religious incantation in place of biology and physics. However, science seems to have failed miserably in the control of the psychosocial environment. Humanity seems to be able to predict and control all of nature except itself. The need to find meaning in existence and emotional peace leads people to seek magic cures. Consequently, witness the continued success of religion, psychotherapy, and other forms of psychofraud.

From a purely emotional point of view, it is clearly preferable to believe that one understands something when one does not, than to admit that one is helpless in coping with an important aspect of nature. In the past, religion filled this need most effectively. However, as science preempted the authority of religion in one field after another, the belief in the traditional religious process itself became shaken. Psychotherapy developed the appearance of rational science without the substance of science. It replaced traditional religious counselling for millions of people (29).* Only when it came to dealing with the seemingly unavoidable problem of death did science and psychotherapy prove less comforting than religion.

THE NEED TO UNDERSTAND

Traditional psychotherapy, by telling persons that their behavior was perfectly understandable in terms of unconscious sexual needs and suppressed desires, created in them the illusion of being able to predict and control their own

* For example, since 1947, the number of primary mental health personnel—psychiatrists, psychotherapists, psychiatric social workers, etc.—has increased from 14,000 to over 100,000 while the number of ministers and priests has decreased from 250,000 to under 200,000.

behavior, and this in turn brought them an inner peace similar to that traditionally provided by religion (42). The behavior of all persons, including entire nations, could be understood, it was alleged, on the basis of psychoanalytic principles (112, 161). Psychotherapeutic principles were applied to child raising, education, industry and many other institutions. Some political leaders underwent extensive treatment. However, after psychotherapy had been in vogue for over fifty years, the problems of society and the individual were getting increasingly worse rather than better. Our constantly expanding mental institutions were filled to overflowing (157). Ten percent or more of the population suffered from mental illness severe enough to require treatment (157). The world was on the brink of destruction through war, pollution, over population and the depletion of resources. The youth revolted and rejected the values of their fathers. Sexual repression became an archaic, historical term. Epidemic venereal disease, resulting from the promiscuous "new morality," was more of a problem. Young men were becoming increasingly impotent (100). Somehow, it did not all fit together. Psychotherapy had been practiced for decades. Sexual liberation was at hand. Yet things seemed to be getting worse—psychotherapy was clearly ineffective. A new magic was needed, one that would appear more compatible with the changing, more entertainment-oriented, affluent life styles in the industrialized countries.

THE NEW MAGIC

The new magic involved a synthesis of the pseudoscience of psychotherapy, mysticism and hedonism. This synthesis was actually begun in the early years of the twentieth century by Jung (70, 161). The hippie movement of the mid-sixties with its drug-induced trances, mystical symbolism and tribalism, found in Jung's philosophy an element of mysticism which could easily be adapted to their chosen lifestyles. From this grew a "new force" called *humanistic psychology*. It is the new magic. It is also psychofraud.

Humanistic psychology combines the rationalism of Freud in the form of Maslow's Psychology of Being (88, 89), with Jung's mystical notions of the collective unconscious, (70) and the youth revolt, to finally take the form of unbridled hedonism. In its final form, it is not only unscientific as were other types of psychotherapy; it is antiscientific.

The old magic required the learning of many complex formulas and incantations. One had to have an M.D. or at least a Ph.D. to be a full-fledged practitioner. The new magic has done away with all this. What matters is not discipline, but relating and feeling. Anyone who is so inclined can set up an "encounter" group where people will come together, feel, and relate. The alleged teachings of a witch doctor, Don Juan, from one of the most primitive Indian tribes in Mexico, are accepted as a new revelation and become the basis of several best-selling books (17, 18). To many, our own culture seems so destructive that surely truth and the way to a better life must be found in the teachings of nonscientific cultures. The possibility that these prescientific cultures are degenerate evolutionary dead ends, which exist only at the sufferance of the scientific cultures, is not considered. These people live in squalor, are ridden with disease, and are scientifically uncreative; yet the followers of the new magic perceive in the primitive societies a comforting wisdom and harmony with nature.

If humanistic psychology has a "spiritual center," it is the Esalen Institute in California, cofounded by the late F. S. Perls, M.D., Ph.D. (179). Here Maslow and many other leaders in humanistic psychology have been residents. A recent and long prominent associate of Esalen is J. C. Lilly, M.D., a neurologist and psychotherapist, whose 1972 book, *The Center of the Cyclone* (83), has been widely praised in major journals by seemingly prominent academicians from leading universities. In the book, Dr. Lilly discusses how after going "beyond science" into mysticism he has communicated through telepathy with beings from other planets, how his trances, induced through drugs and apparent brain damage, led him to meet his guardian angels, and how he had the mystical experience of giving birth to himself while having a massive bowel movement. It is a very popular book which has gone through many printings and has been taken quite seriously. According to Dr. Lilly, it is his intent to guide persons into higher realms of wisdom.

Although classical psychotherapy will continue to attract practitioners and older patients, the future almost surely belongs to the new magic. For by totally rejecting the need for logical coherence in dealing with the psychosocial environment, it has preempted both religion and therapy. Since religion and psychotherapy both derive their effectiveness from faith rather than scientific evidence, a new system of psychoreligious therapy which fulfills mystical, emotional and hedonistic needs with less intellectual effort on the part of both patient and therapist and for less money will prove to be the most popular new form of entertainment. It is psychofraud in its most effective guise to date.

THE NEED FOR AN ALTERNATIVE

If psychofraud makes people so happy, why should we fight it? Why not just give in to it and enjoy ourselves? Our so-called "scientific cultures" really have become destructive. What good is scientific progress if it leads to annihilation? These questions do not have simple answers. The answers will be explored in detail with the development of the Ethical Theory in Part Two. We will consider briefly what has happened to the unscientific, psychofraudulent cultures of the past.

Without exception, the psychofraudulent cultures of the past have stagnated, decayed and been replaced by stronger, more progressive ones. The pattern seems to be that when a new culture starts, it is technologically progressive. This progress brings wealth to the people, or at least to the leaders. Once the culture becomes wealthy, it becomes uncreative and turns increasingly to psychofraud for entertainment. The people then begin an intellectual and ethical decline, and they are replaced by a poorer but still dynamic culture. This happened when the Chaldeans replaced the Summerians and were in turn replaced by the Persians. This happened when the Hellenes replaced the Minoans and then the Persians and were in turn replaced by the Romans, who decayed in the same way.

It happened in India when the Aryans replaced the Dravidians. It happened on the world scale when the United States at the end of World War II replaced the European powers as the center of scientific and technological creativity. The psychofrauds of Europe were fascism and communism. The psychofraud gestating in the United States is the new magic: humanistic psychology and neomysticism.

We probably cannot have another great civilization collapse through psychofraud and still continue human evolution. This is the case because of the nature of modern weapons, the rapidly depleting natural resources which are irreplaceable, the interdependent net of modern technology, and the possibility of a world police state which stifles all progress (50).

The problems created by science can only be solved by science. Science works. It is the very real effectiveness of science which is threatening to destroy all life on earth. The problems which science causes are not inherent to the nature of science but to man himself, who uses science for predicting and controlling the physical and the biological environments, but uses psychofraud to predict and control his own behavior. It is not because man cannot predict and control the external world that science has become a menace, but because he cannot predict and control himself.

The creative prediction and control of human behavior is

the purpose of Ethical Therapy and scientific ethics in general. However, this is also the stated purpose of many forms of psychofraud. In order to distinguish between methods which are scientific and those which are psychofraudulent, it is necessary to understand both psychofraud and science. In order to use science creatively, it is necessary to develop an objective system of ethics which does not lead to scientific contradictions as do most of the traditional ethical systems. Psychofraud is the major impediment to the development of scientific ethics, because psychofraud can make us happy in the absence of truth. Psychofraud makes it easy to avoid unpleasant realities by providing us with comforting illusions.

We can find temporary happiness in psychofraud, but reality cannot be avoided forever. If it does not catch up with us, it will catch up with our children. For this reason we need a scientific, ethical alternative to psychofraud if we have any concern at all with the future. Even for those who care for nothing beyond their personal happiness, Ethical Therapy is a better alternative because it will maximize their happiness (50). However, we cannot begin to use Ethical Therapy until we begin to understand the fatal attraction of psychofraud.

2

A Fatal Attraction

After thousands of years of experiencing psychofraud and seeing it repeatedly exposed, one would think that humanity would have learned to distrust and avoid it. However, psychofraud is still with us and growing. In the past it was mostly religious in nature, but the advent and success of systematic science has caused it to acquire pseudoscientific trappings. We can see this in the so-called scientific socialism of Marxism, which is no more scientific than Thomistic theology and considerably less rigorous (50).

The current surge of interest in "scientific" astrology is even more bewildering. Astrology has been practiced for thousands of years. One would think that if there were anything to it, someone would have put it to practical use by now and used astrological "science" to rule the world or at least make a killing on the stock market. Hitler tried to use astrological "science" in lieu of sound military strategy. The results are history. Yet many thousands of apparently intelligent people take astrology seriously. Nevertheless, it is in the social "sciences" that psychofraud seems to have its most pernicious effects.

SOCIAL "SCIENCE"

The purpose of any science is to predict and control the environment with which it is concerned. Social science is concerned with human behavior. If social "science" were truly scientific, it could be scientifically demonstrated. Yet we see that other than by physical coercion and primitive conditioning techniques, humanity seems to have been quite ineffective in predicting and controlling its own behavior. For example, the most rigorous and quantitative social "science" is economics. Yet we see famous economic "experts" giving contradictory advice on all important subjects and making dismally wrong predictions. We see political and social systems turned upside down to accommodate some economic theory. Still the economic predictions turn out to be in serious error.

The psychotherapists tell us how to raise mentally healthy children with the use of psychotherapeutic principles. Several generations of children were raised this way. Yet the number of mental patients skyrockets (157). There seems to be no discernable beneficial effect from incorporating psychotherapeutic principles into our culture.

The principles of scientific method are well understood. Many social "scientists" give them lip service (137, 138); yet they are not used except in the most trivial and banal cases. The really important problems of how to increase human creativity and well-being are almost never treated scientifically, i.e., knowledge of these problems is not developed systematically on the basis of experiments with placebo and other controls. Why not?

The first answer that comes to mind is that there are so many interacting variables influencing social phenomena that it is not possible to do controlled experiments. However, if we look at the psychosocial theories, we see that these are very simple theories which explain complex behavioral phenomena on the basis of a few simple hypotheses. The following, simplified examples, represent the distillation to their essential components of four psychosocial theories which are currently affecting millions of human lives.

Example 1. "Capitalism is the source of all human misery. Eliminate all forms of private ownership; concentrate all the means of production in the public's hands and we will automatically create a paradise on earth." Yet communist countries are not exactly paradises, particularly for creative persons.

Example 2. "Unequal scholastic performance is due to unequal educational opportunity. Equalize the educational opportunity and all children will perform equally well in school." Yet we know that this does not happen. Reflect on the large numbers of children with wealthy parents, who are scholastic failures, and the large number of poor children who are outstanding achievers, such as Joseph Haydn, Benjamin Franklin, Alexander Hamilton, Abraham Lincoln, Booker T. Washington, Mark Twain, H. G. Wells, G. B. Shaw, and the eminent black American mathematician, David Blackwell (68, 69, 98).

Example 3. "There can be no neuroses if a person has a normal sex life. Create an environment where people can have a full and uninhibited sex life and we will eliminate all forms of neuroses." This is clearly not the case. Sex has been increasingly freely and openly discussed and practiced; yet by all accounts, neuroses are increasing (157).

Example 4. "Human behavior is nothing but a series of conditioned responses. Give me the specifications and a child at birth, and I will give you the specified adult." This latter ideology of the behaviorist school of psychology has clearly not worked; to date, not a single behaviorist has produced an outstanding creative genius among his children. Indeed their children seem to be on the whole as ordinary as their parents. Behaviorism will be discussed in greater detail later.

What all these separate and distinct social science theories and ideologies have in common is that (1) they each seem to contain elements of truth, (2) they grossly oversimplify the actual case, and (3) they are accepted as true without experimental proof. It is the human tendency to grossly oversimplify reality and not verify by objective experimentation that engenders psychofraud in social science. The interconnectedness of all causative factors must be considered if a psychosocial theory is to reflect reality.

THE SEARCH FOR SIMPLICITY

As was discussed earlier, human beings seem to have an innate need to predict and control their total environment. When a situation is not understood, the simplest feasible explanation which makes the person feel that he now has some understanding, i.e., ability to predict and control, will be accepted. To primitive man, the simplest explanation was that the universe was inhabited by spirits who caused all the natural phenomena he saw, just as the phenomena of his own body was caused by his spirit, which inhabited his body and which he perceived directly. This theory did not enable him to predict and control very much, but it gave him some peace of mind and enabled him to think he understood and could control nature through magic and prayers.

As more complex and more scientific models of the universe were developed, humanity became better able to predict its total environment. However, knowledge is such that we cannot learn to better predict and control one aspect of the environment without almost simultaneously learning of a new aspect of the environment which was previously unknown and therefore unpredictable to us. For example, the development of classical physics (Newtonian mechanics, optics, the electromagnetic theory, etc.) led to our technological civilization. Technological civilization in turn caused problems of pollution, industrial exploitation, weapons of mass destruction, overpopulation, etc. The increase of knowledge in classical physics led to modern physics (relativity, field theory, quantum mechanics, etc.) which, in the words of J. G. S. Haldane, indicate "that the universe is not only queerer than we imagine, but queerer than we can imagine." *Deus non est machina.* Darwin's theory of evolution and its modern forms, molecular biology, and mathematical genetics have destroyed the simple view of individual, unique creation for each life-form and shown that there is a continuum of complexity from matter to life and that man has more in common with other life-forms than he thought (96). We are now aware of the incredible biophysical complexities of life, as, in the past, we did not even conceive of these complexities, but regarded life-forms as units.

Biophysical neurophysiology indicates that there is a one-to-one relationship between mind states and brain states (13, 15, 125, 139, 149). However, we are just beginning to explore the complexity of the human brain, which is the most complex aspect of life known to man. As we begin to better understand the brain and the nature of mental fields, a whole new universe of incredible complexity will be discovered, and we will once again realize that as our knowledge of the universe grows, so does our knowledge of our ignorance.

It has been said that (1) the wisest man is the man who knows and knows he knows, (2) the next wisest man is the man who knows but does not know he knows, (3) the third wisest man is the man who does not know and knows he does not know, and (4) the most ignorant man is the man who does not know but thinks he knows. The last man is a victim of psychofraud. Most of humanity has been in this latter category for thousands of years. True knowledge begins only when we begin to doubt our knowledge.

Humanity has a dilemma. It cannot acquire true knowledge without at the same time becoming more aware of its own ignorance. It is much more comforting to have pseudo-knowledge, which gives a simple explanation of everything in the universe and keeps us ignorant of our own ignorance, than to have true knowledge, which makes us aware of how much we still have to learn.

Religion, for example, explains everything in the universe and makes those who accept it feel that they have nothing more of real importance to learn. It is only when someone shows that he can predict and control better than religion in some aspect of the environment that religious foundations begin to crumble. Since religion cannot compete with science in effectiveness, it continuously narrows its focus to those parts of the total environment which have not yet yielded to the scientific method.

This begins with the physical environment. Where prayer was once used to ward off physical disaster, science explains, predicts and eventually enables us to control everything from tempests to eclipses and earthquakes. As the scientific ability to predict and control increases, people rely less and less on religious means for dealing with these phenomena. Persons may, at present, now pray to avoid disaster in an earthquake, but they will no longer do this when science learns how to predict and control earthquakes. Similarly, man once prayed for rain, but he ceased to so do when he learned to control it by cloud seeding. People used to pray for their health during plague epidemics. Now, if they are sensible, they merely get inoculated. However, this increasing ability to predict and control has opened a Pandora's box of new problems.

PANDORA'S BOX

Once man chose a scientific way of coping with nature, he became increasingly dependent on science for his very survival. Try as he would, he could not for long avoid reality, or his technological civilization would collapse, and he would perish along with it (50). Yet the truly important questions—Who am I? Where am I going? What is the meaning of my existence? How can human beings live together in a progressive society?—seem to have been left unanswered by science. Still there was no shortage of psychofraudulent ideologies which claimed to answer them. Man continued to cling to comforting ideologies and accept new ones when they were more attractive or logically consistent than the existing systems.

It is this need to cling to the illusion of certainty, while science continues to increase the uncertainty in the world by posing ever more complex problems, that is at the core of the recent resurgence of psychofraud and the moral dilemma that threatens to destroy the human race. By choosing science as a means of predicting and controlling its physical environment, humanity, without knowing it, opened a Pandora's Box of ever new problems which are created by the very success of physical science.

With considerable effort, mankind managed to extend science to biology in the nineteenth century. Reflect on the opposition to Darwin's theory and its modern variants in all countries. The extension of science to biology in the nineteenth century was done at the cost of man's image of himself as a specially created being for whom a good and merciful god has special concern. Darwin's theory of evolution and its modern extensions, which show man evolving not only from apelike creatures, but from elementary matter through *random* occurrences, have destroyed any rational person's view of man as a special object of divine creation. The knowledge that the earth is less than a mote of dust in a virtually limitless universe and that man is entirely on his own in it without any guarantees from anyone has opened an abyss before humanity into which few wish to look.

THE ABYSS

The abyss results from the knowledge that we may have evolved, not according to some divine plan, but through a series of *random accidents* which led to the survival of the strong at the price of the extinction of the weak (96). It is not the meek that have inherited the earth, but the most bloodthirsty predatory animal in history—man. No other animal has ever systematically slaughtered its own kind in countless millions for the sheer pleasure it brings. No other animal has brought so many thousands of species to extinction or near extinction. No other animal has ever threatened to destroy all life on earth.

To look into the abyss is to see ourselves as we are. To see ourselves as we are is to look at the face of death in a seemingly purposeless and indifferent universe. Most men seek to avoid this confrontation and thus blind themselves with psychofraud. However, it is only by confronting the reality of what and why we are that we can overcome our fears and begin to cope with ourselves as effectively as we have with the physical and biological environments. It is the purpose of Ethical Therapy to cure us of this self-imposed blindness.

BLINDNESS

Since the end of World War II, man has lived under a Damoclean sword of nuclear annihilation. Annihilation became a popular topic of public discourse for presidents, statesmen and ordinary men. It was a recurrent theme in popular fiction, films and theater. No less than 2000 works of fiction pertaining to nuclear annihilation have been published since the end of World War II. Yet today this subject is virtually ignored by both public and private men. It is no longer a topic for any fiction that sells. Why is this?

A cynic would say that the market became glutted by apocalyptic writings and speeches. Nuclear annihilation simply does not sell any more. An optimist would say that we now have a more stable balance of power and nuclear annihilation is not nearly the threat that it was in the early 1960s. A realist would note the following.

There is greater danger of nuclear annihilation today than

there ever was. Until the early 1960s, only the United States had the capacity to totally destroy its enemies. Today both the United States and the Soviets have the capacity to destroy the entire human race several times over. Furthermore, these weapon systems are becoming increasingly destructive and automated. The men controlling them, if anything, are more venal and ignorant than those who controlled them in the past (50). The so-called balance of power merely makes the situation more unstable because there no longer is any single power with the capacity to absolutely impose its will on the other. Furthermore, this instability is increasing as new nations—China, France, Israel, Japan, India—acquire nuclear capability. The weapons grow in destructiveness and proliferate even as the capacity of our political leaders to deal with the situation diminishes. This is not stability, but increasing instability. The avoidance of the issue is not due to the fact that it does not exist or that it is no longer relevant, but rather to the fact that it is a fearsome subject with which we seem to have lost the capacity to cope. The Freudians would call this issue-avoidance "repression."

The repression of the knowledge of the obvious danger from nuclear annihilation seems to have begun shortly after the confrontation between the United States and the Soviet Union over the Cuban Missile Crisis in 1962. At this time, the world came so close to actual nuclear war that it seemed to produce a type of psychic shock which could only be overcome by self-imposed blindness. Although some major films on the nuclear annihilation theme, such as *Fail Safe* and *Dr. Strangelove*, were made after this period, the number of original writings on the theme began to diminish. The unconscious expression of anxiety through art is the last to be suppressed. *Dr. Strangelove* put an end to the whole affair by treating this very serious matter as a comedy. It is a common defense mechanism to laugh and joke at situations with which we can no longer cope. By the beginning of the 1970s, nuclear annihilation was simply no longer a subject that could be discussed on any level with the vast majority of people. Mankind had totally repressed its fears of nuclear annihilation. The problem was simply ignored. This was self-imposed blindness to reality (50). It was psychofraud.

A danger similar in scope to nuclear annihilation, but not quite as imminent, is that of pollution. Although films about nuclear annihilation are no longer popular, films about ecological disaster are still being made, e.g., *The Omega Man*, *Silent Running*, and *Soylent Green*. After deep concern was expressed with the ecological crises in the late sixties, the public began to lose conscious concern with it as soon as the magnitude of the problem became clear. The unconscious concern remained in art forms as in the case of films, but eventually even this will disappear as in the case of nuclear annihilation. There seemed no way of adequately coping with the problem through existing bureaucratic systems. It was clear that if we did not cope with it, the situation could become irreversible. Eventually, we would not be able to avoid annihilation by pollution even with our best efforts (50). Therefore, the reality of this danger began to be suppressed by psychofraud just as nuclear danger had been suppressed.

The psychofraud in this case was that man could avoid ecological disaster by returning to a simple, prescientific, pastoral existence and by rejecting science and technology.* The same phenomena is occurring in all the danger areas confronting humanity—ranging from genetic decay through the elimination of natural selection among the human species, to the significance of massive drug addiction and

* This view, of course, ignores the fact that the world could not support its present population without the aid of science and technology and that the destruction of our technological civilization would lead to mass starvation and worse conditions. See *The Greening of America* by Charles Reich as an example of this type of psychofraud.

growing hedonism among young persons. When men cannot cope with an important problem, they blind themselves to it through psychofraud.

VARIETIES OF PSYCHOFRAUD

Psychofraud occurs whenever a person cannot face up to his own ignorance and impotence. It is psychologically more comforting to *believe* that one understands than to know that one does not know. It is more comforting to imagine a world in which we can predict and control than to live in a world in which we cannot cope with reality. Depending on the vigor of his imagined fantasies, a person is classified either as a neurotic or a psychotic. A well-known psychiatrist once related the following parable of the neuroses-psychoses dimension: "Neurotics build castles in the sky, psychotics live in them, and psychotherapists collect rent from both."

Here we see the full dimension of psychofraud from comforting illusions to complete and often disastrous distortions of reality. Reality includes both that which we can predict and control and that which we cannot predict and control. So long as we can predict and control our own thoughts, we can escape from having to confront the world outside our thoughts. By creating fantasies we *can* predict and control our own thoughts. If we are not imaginative enough to create our own fantasies, for a price someone else will create them for us. They will help us build the imaginary castles, live in them, and then collect rent from us. This "helper" may be a psychiatrist, a priest or a political ideologue. We accept their guidance because the thoughts they engender are much more satisfactory than those engendered by reality or our own fantasies.

It is the innate need to predict and control which drives us toward both greater knowledge and self-delusion. However, illusions cannot be maintained indefinitely. Reality will eventually overtake us, if not as individuals, then as a species. The moral choice is either to face reality with all its concomitant horror and loneliness or to find happiness in temporary illusion. The only way we know what is real is by *scientifically* testing our theories to see if in fact they truly enable us to predict and control. It is not our *belief* in our abilities to predict and control that counts, but whether in fact we *actually do* predict and control.

The mystic has complete confidence in his knowledge, i.e., his ability to predict and control the world around him, without ever having subjected this belief to a test. It is his inner conviction, his personal enlightenment, that counts. Therefore, most mystics concentrate on predicting and controlling their own thoughts, for only in the mind can fantasies find complete insulation from reality. If the mystic can discipline his mind to ignore the fact that he lives in filth, that his children and brothers are dying of disease, and that the beautiful thoughts that he creates will all die with his body, then the mystic has reached the true Nirvana. Entire civilizations have been built on this belief in mystical enlightenment.

We need only walk through the streets of Calcutta covered with the excrement of the deformed, dying or already dead bodies which line the sidewalks, to see the logical conclusion of the mystical approach to truth. Half the world has turned toward mysticism. It lives in contentment among its own decay, kept alive by the food, medicine and technology produced by the nations with a scientific culture. The youth of the United States and other affluent democracies, confronted with the horror of their own existence, have come to envy the contentment of the mystical degenerates and are beginning to emulate them. But it is a prosperous, technological civilization which makes it possible for them to temporarily avoid reality.

In the communist countries, on the other hand, the mystical approach to life is severely repressed. Here the psychofraud is political, not mystical. It consists in the belief that man is nothing more than organized matter and that the founders and current leaders of the communist society have *scientifically* learned how to predict and control human evolution. The fact that communist theory has made very poor predictions of historical events in the twentieth century is ignored and suppressed whenever possible. Any critic of the system is killed, imprisoned or driven insane in political asylums (176). The whole society is structured to avoid the unpleasant fact that there is more to reality than is explained by communist ideology. The whole society seems to become insane, and the sane are put in asylums. All of humanity's social creations seem to end up as means for maintaining illusions of certainty.

In the industrialized Western democracies, the greatest uncertainties plaguing the population are uncertainties about their own emotions and mental processes. Having largely eliminated the uncertainties of infectious diseases, inadequate shelter and poor diet, together with the uncertainties of being subject to the whims of capricious tyrants, the people in the progressive democracies have become obsessed with their own psyches. Having used science and technology to cope effectively with the physical and biological environments, the people have become obsessed with the uncertainties of the psychosocial environment. Because the basic physical and biological problems have been solved, attention is focused on emotional problems and the psychosocial environment. Instead of extending the scientific method to this new aspect of the environment, the population succumbs to psychofraud (43, 48, 83, 106).

We succumb to psychofraud because mysticism, psychotherapy and the social sciences give us *immediate* answers on how to cope with the psychosocial environment. The facts that these "answers" (1) have not been subject to experimental verification and (2) are not based on scientifically developed data are ignored in a desperate attempt to make sense out of a miserable life in a disintegrating society. The easy promises of certainty offered by psychofraud eventually overcome any lingering skepticism.

The need for certainty is the fatal flaw in human nature. This is what must be overcome through Ethical Therapy. Humanity must learn to cope with the insecurity of "uncertainty." It must learn to see itself in a perspective of awesome cosmic reality. It must learn to live with doubt and danger in an infinite universe whose nature can never be fully understood. Humanity must progress without knowing toward what it is progressing. If not, it will destroy itself by self-imposed blindness to the dangers which it itself creates. Whether our species is capable of making this ethical transformation is itself uncertain.

THE CHOICE

The choice before each person is simple yet profound. Will I live to increase happiness or truth? Happiness and truth are not mutually exclusive, but neither are they identical. The importance is in which one of these two states we choose as our goal for making decisions. Psychofraud can make persons happy and relieve anxiety, but it cannot increase truth. Increasing truth can cause unhappiness for anyone who is a practitioner or a victim of psychofraud. However, it is only when we seek truth for its own sake that we can be truly happy (50).

We cannot learn when we are certain. Only those who doubt learn. Yet doubt itself makes most persons unhappy. However, this is only the case when happiness is seen as the ultimate goal of existence. When truth for its own sake is our final goal, then we are always happy. That this is the case can be shown logically and experimentally (50). However, victims of psychofraud will not surrender their illusions to reason. They will do everything in their power to avoid any scientific evidence that will cause doubt and end the security of certainty. They will seek to avoid the responsibility that they have for their evolution and that of their fellowman. This emotional need for psychofraud and all encompassing ideologies is what must be overcome. The choice before everyone is whether to accept or reject psychofraud. The choice is whether to be happy in our illusions or to grow in objective truth.

The institutions most concerned with helping persons overcome psychofraud are themselves the worst victims of psychofraud. This applies to our schools and universities (50), but most of all to the psychotherapeutic community. Today the psychotherapists are the main *practitioners* of psychofraud as well as its worst *victims*.

3

Psychotherapy

Psychotherapy is the oldest type of medical practice. Any administration of a placebo is a form of psychotherapy; and almost all of medical practice, until very recent years, has consisted mainly in the administration of placebos or, what is worse, harmful (iatrogenic) treatments (73, 153). However, when the concern was with "aberrant" behavior, as opposed to some obvious physical condition, then a form of psychofraud was usually used to change the aberrant behavior.

The anthropological evidence indicates that throughout most of his history, man used various forms of sympathetic magic for coping with this behavior (44). During recorded history the most common theory explaining aberrant behavior was possession by demons. Even nondestructive, but highly creative, behavior led to the suspicion that the person was in league with the devil or some other demons, e.g., the Faust legend. The Bible, New Testament and Old, is full of formulae for coping with possession by devils. The resurgence of psychofraud has brought about a new popular concern with Satanism and demonology (146).

During the Middle Ages and as late as the eighteenth century, everything from witchcraft to homosexuality came under the heading of "unnatural acts" caused by demonic possession or alliance (153, 154). The Inquisition would burn at the stake protestants, witches, and homosexuals with equal aplomb. All were considered heretics. The theory was that in order to drive the demon(s) out, the heretic must be forced to confess his sins, by torture if necessary, in order that his soul might be saved. It was better that the body perish in order that the immoral soul might live in heaven forever. Although this practice continued on a wide scale until the eighteenth century, the age of reason finally caught up with mental illness.

In 1716, there was published in England a modern rational attempt to explain mental aberrations. The rational theory propounded at this time, which was to survive more than two hundred years as an orthodox teaching, was that insanity was caused not by supernatural demons, an obvious "superstition," but by masturbation.* In time, virtually all aberrant behavior was to be explained by the masturbatory hypothesis. Benjamin Rush, "The Father of American Psychiatry," and a signer of the Declaration of Independence, was a full-fledged proponent of the concept of masturbatory insanity. Even so eminent a psychiatrist as Ernest Jones, the pupil and biographer of Sigmund Freud, could state in 1918 that "true neurasthenia . . . will be found to depend on excessive onanism or involuntary seminal emission" (153).

During the late nineteenth century and the early twentieth century, it was a common medical practice among "progressive" circles to cauterize with red-hot irons or amputate the clitoris of girls found masturbating "to excess" (153). It was argued that it was better to lose a clitoris than to become insane. Boys who masturbated "to excess" had the dorsal nerves of the penis removed. This might make them im-

* Superstition is defined as the religious beliefs of *others.*

potent, but supposedly it saved them from the insane asylum.

Although the classical Freudians regarded masturbation as abnormal, they did not, with the exception of Ernest Jones, consider it the major cause of mental illness, but rather as a contributing factor or side effect of improper sexual development. They still thought the major source of mental illness to be of a sexual nature, but they did not advocate clitorectomies. Psychoanalysis was a less drastic placebo for preventing insanity. It formed the basis of most modern forms of psychotherapy and psychofraud. However, the Freudians were not the end to the gross physical mutilation of human beings to prevent aberrant behavior.

In 1938, Egas Moniz, a Portuguese physician, developed the operation known as a *lobotomy* to deal with aberrant behavior. This operation, in which the nerves to the frontal lobes of the brain are destroyed, was so effective in calming persons, removing anxiety and making them docile, that it became the "in" operation of café society. Physicians were performing this operation in their offices. One physician alone did 1500 of them (153). Yet when lobotomies were subjected to scientific analysis, they were shown to provide no lasting benefits (153). They calmed persons down at the cost of destroying their imagination and turning them into vegetables. Still Egas Moniz was awarded the 1955 Nobel Prize in medicine for his "great" discovery. Today, there is a resurgence of psychosurgery after the eclipse brought about by tranquilizing drugs.

Tranquilizers are in many ways chemical lobotomies, apparently without the permanent deleterious side effects of surgical lobotomies. In a recent experiment in Massachusetts (108), it was shown that the only effective form of treatment for chronic schizophrenics was the use of tranquilizers and other drugs. None of the traditional forms of psychotherapy, even when applied by some of the most "illustrious" psychiatrists in Massachusetts, seemed to have any differential effect.

Clearly drugs have an effect on the central nervous system

which can produce behavioral changes. Drug therapy, however, is no longer generally considered a form of psychotherapy. *Psychotherapy has come to refer primarily to a change in the information content of the central nervous system and not necessarily to a direct change in its physiology or biochemical structure.*

There is no precise definition of psychotherapy; however, the following are commonly used:

—a technique for bringing about mental changes that reduce anxiety and increase a person's ability to cope with life.

—the art and science of psychic healing.

—the technique of remedying or alleviating mental disorders.

—the science for modifying and correcting aberrant behavior.

The above definitions, while having some intuitive appeal, could include everything from Christian Science to astrology. We must have more objective, precise definitions, if we are to make meaningful comparisons between different forms of psychotherapy. The best way to begin is to discuss mental health, neuroses and psychoses.

MENTAL HEALTH

It is ironic that with the notable exception of Maslow and a few others (26, 89, 90), leading psychotherapists have concentrated on describing mental disease without first describing mental health. If any process is to be able to treat disease effectively, we should have a clear notion of what the end goal is. This end goal, a healthy person, should be the common goal of all therapy, mental or physical.

Let us assume that we are medical students in some school of the future. We are given two persons to examine. We are told that one is healthier than the other. We must find out which one this is. To simplify the problem, let us assume that our patients are identical twins.

First we give our patients a complete physical examination —height, weight, blood tests, urine analysis, electrocardiograms, electroencephalograms, skin tests, etc. When we have finished these tests, we find that both patients are identical in every measurement. We must then conclude, if we trust our physical examination techniques, that it is in mental, and not physical, health that the patients differ. Therefore, we give them a whole battery of so-called mental tests which allegedly measure personality and intellectual differences. Again, we find that the two patients have identical responses.

Being sophisticated about mental tests, we do not take them as seriously as the physical tests. We guess that our patients might have been coached by our examiners in how to respond to these tests in order to make the problem more difficult for us. However, we have been given an extended amount of time in which to finish our examination. Since the twins share a house and they are at our mercy in everything except having to tell us the truth, we decide to move in with them and observe their everyday behavior.

We find that both twins have identical educations, received identical grades in school, and hold identical jobs as engineers at separate branches of a large corporation. When we check the personnel records of the corporation we find that twin A has received several bonuses for having designed new machines. He is almost never ill. Twin B, while doing a satisfactory job, has not invented anything and has only received a conventional cost-of-living and seniority increase. He has had four colds during the last year which caused him to be absent from work. When we interview the co-workers of the twins, we find that the co-workers of twin A have considerable affection and respect for him; while the co-workers of twin B do not particularly like or dislike him, they merely find him tolerable.

After living with the twins for a week, we see that twin A is engaged to an intelligent, charming and beautiful woman. He often gets telephone calls from female and male friends. He is very good at sports and practices them to stay fit. Twin B, on the other hand, has no friends of either sex, and spends much of his nonworking time watching television and reading pornographic magazines. He does not engage in physical activity. He tries to meet women, but he seems to have trouble getting dates. At this time, we might begin to suspect that twin A is the healthier of the two. Why is this?

A first intuitive reason is that with identical intellectual and physical equipment, twin A is better able to cope with his environment than twin B. Twin A is more creative in his work and his social relationships. Twin B seems to engage in a more escapist, uncreative activity. We might be wrong, but our guess is that twin A is healthier because he can better predict and control his total environment—physical, biological and psychosocial.

Twin A shows his superior ability to predict and control his (1) physical environment through his engineering innovations, (2) biological environment through freedom from illness and athletic prowess, and (3) psychosocial environment through successful social relationships with members of both sexes. *Our basic criterion for health is, therefore, the ability to predict and control the total environment—physical, biological and psychosocial.*

In actual practice we may not find such clear-cut distinctions between persons. Those who are highly capable in the physical environment might be deficient in the psychosocial environment and vice-versa. Therefore, the concept of health is a weighted measure in which the ability to predict and control in each main dimension of the environment must be weighed relative to the ability to predict and control in the other two dimensions.

As will be shown in Part Two and is shown elsewhere (50), the healthiest person can predict, control and, above all, create equally well in all dimensions of the total environment. He never becomes highly proficient in one dimension while remaining totally incapable in the other dimensions.

MENTAL ILLNESS

If health is measured by a person's ability to predict and control his total environment and his creativity, then illness is anything that decreases either our ability to predict and control any aspect of our environment or to create. This agrees with many of our intuitive notions of illness. For example, colds, cancer, and syphilis are, intuitively speaking, diseases. They also decrease our ability to predict, control and create. Other more controversial mental and physical states, such as homosexuality, mental deficiency and racial prejudice, would also be classified as illness under our criterion because they decrease our ability to predict and control; homosexuality, by reducing our ability to bear and raise children; mental deficiency, by reducing our ability to learn and cope with nature in general. Other things being equal, the more intelligent a person, the healthier he is. We define intelligence as "the ability to predict and control the total environment—physical, biological and psychosocial."

Racial prejudice is a mental state not usually considered a disease, but by our criterion of mental health, it is, because it diminishes our ability to learn and cooperate with those races toward whom we are antagonistic. We lose the capacity to evaluate each person on the basis of his individual merit, and this decreases our ability to predict and control our psychosocial environment.

The prediction and control criteria for health apply equally well whether we are speaking of purely mental or purely physical health. A person who has lost a leg will, by and large, have his ability to predict and control his total environment diminished, though not necessarily equally in all dimensions. This is obvious in the physical and biological environment. In the psychosocial environment the effect will be more subtle and will result from the fact that many persons tend to treat amputees as less than complete human beings. This is a result of neuroses on their part, not that of the amputee. However, it will still tend to diminish the amputee's ability to predict and control his psychosocial environment.

If a person has a purely mental problem, such as a paranoidal obsession that every human being is a plotting, treacherous cheat who wishes to swindle him and cause him harm, this will decrease his ability to predict and control his total environment. He will be defensive and uncreative in his social relationships because he cannot trust or work with anyone. He will be ineffective in the biological environment because he will regard medical personnel as persons who only wish to take his money without providing any real service; this will cause his health to suffer. He will diminish his effectiveness and creativity in the physical environment by spending more of his time seeking to protect himself from the evil intentions of others than in trying to learn as much science and technology as he can.

These are, of course, extreme examples to illustrate a point. However, the same type of analysis applies to any type of physical or mental disorder. When mental disorders are serious, they are called "psychoses." When they are less serious, they are called "neuroses."

Psychoses

A common definition of psychoses is the following:

> *A person is psychotic when he cannot distinguish between imagined stimuli and real stimuli.*

We can all imagine a poisonous scorpion climbing up our leg. Our response to this imagined scorpion is quite different than that to a real scorpion. To a psychotic, the imaginary and the real scorpion are regarded as equally real, and he responds accordingly.

A more common and in some ways more dangerous type of psychosis exists when one imagines that certain real stimuli do not exist. In this case, if a real scorpion is crawling up his leg, because the reality is so horrible, he imagines that it is not there and does nothing to avoid the danger. Similar types of psychoses are induced by severe trauma, e.g., "shell shock" in battle. They may also be socially contagious, as when a whole nation ignores an obvious danger to itself. Clearly, all forms of psychoses are self-imposed cases of psychofraud. One might call this "autopsychofraud."

These extreme cases of autopsychofraud are usually due to organic causes, such as acute alcoholism, LSD, vitamin B deficiency, and brain damage. There is considerable evidence that many cases of extreme psychotic behavior have a genetic origin and owe little or nothing to environmental circumstances (117). That is to say, some persons are born with some biochemical or physiological disorder that predisposes them to psychotic behavior. For example, there is a clear hereditary pattern in schizophrenia, which is the most common form of psychosis (117).

The clearly organic factors involved in psychoses are also demonstrated by the measurable differences in the blood biochemistry of schizophrenics. It seems that some schizophrenics possess an active substance in their blood similar in its biochemistry and physiological effects to LSD. When this substance is isolated and injected into normal persons, it can produce psychotic symptoms (11, 75, 125, 127, 139, 140). Other forms of schizophrenia seem to be quite amenable to treatment with massive doses of vitamins. It has been shown that some schizophrenics can assimilate up to 1000 times the normal vitamin C dose.

Psychosis, as might be expected, is highly resistant to treatment by psychotherapy or psychofraud. Placebos do not seem to work very well, although there can be some placebo effect. Modern psychogenic drugs, such as tranquilizers, seem to have definite effects in controlling psychotic behavior (73, 108). However, they do not seem to have creative effects. That is to say, psychotics can be made to stop their most destructive behavior through the use of drugs, but they cannot significantly increase their ability to predict and control the total environment. Conditioning techniques, such as those practiced by the behaviorists, can also slightly improve schizophrenic behavior. But, like drugs, those treatments do not seem to increase creativity.

In nonpsychotic persons, drugs such as alcohol, LSD and marijuana can create the illusion that persons have increased their ability to predict and control. There is no objective evidence that this is truly the case. There is considerable evidence indicating the opposite case (177). There have been several cases of persons who, while under the influence of LSD, thought they could fly and jumped to their deaths from high buildings. The so-called mind-expanding drugs are therefore a particularly pernicious form of psychofraud, which induce psychotic or neurotic symptoms.

Neuroses

The differences between psychoses and neuroses are primarily quantitative, not qualitative. Neurosis is commonly defined as follows:

> *A person is neurotic if he has anxieties and emotions which interfere with his ability to accomplish his purposes.*

Clearly all psychotics fit the definition of a neurotic. Indeed, virtually all human beings are or have been neurotic by this definition. In our concept of mental health, psychoses and neuroses are on a continuum. At one end of this continuum is the extreme psychotic, who has so distorted reality that his behavior could quickly cause him to die or kill others on impulse if he is left unattended. At the other extreme is the mild neurotic, who may make occasional errors in judgment because of emotional factors which decrease his ability to predict and control. In the previous example, twin B appeared more neurotic than twin A, although both may have been neurotic by our definition.

Another distinction that can be made is that while psychotic behavior seems to be due primarily to organic causes and cannot be significantly altered by nonorganic means, neurotic behavior seems to be almost entirely learned and is susceptible to modification by any type of psychofraud whether placebos, religion, political ideology, or astrology. For our purposes we will make the following definition of all maladaptive (neurotic) behavior:

> *Neurosis (neurotic behavior) is any learned pattern of behavior which decreases a person's ability to predict and control his total environment.*

The fact that neurotic behavior is learned does not preclude there being an organic predisposition in some persons which makes them more susceptible to neuroses than others. Under this classification, psychotics have a very strong organic predisposition caused by heredity, drugs, or physical trauma which makes them highly susceptible to learning neurotic behavior. In fact, they can learn little else. Any person can eventually be made neurotic if he is exposed to the proper learning experiences. However, unlearned experiences, such as physical or chemical brain damage, which decrease our ability to predict and control are not neuroses, but merely illnesses. It will be shown in Part Two that only persons who have successfully undergone Ethical Therapy are totally devoid of neuroses and cannot be made neurotic except possibly by the forced administration of drugs or psychosurgery.

PSYCHOTHERAPY DEFINED

> *Psychotherapy is any technique which corrects neurotic patterns of behavior. That is to say, psychotherapy is a technique for replacing old learned patterns of neurotic behavior with newly learned patterns of behavior which increase a person's ability to predict and*

control his total environment—physical, biological and psychosocial. Psychotherapy is a special kind of education.

Education is any process which teaches us new ways of better predicting and controlling our total environment. What makes psychotherapy special is that it replaces a learned neurotic pattern of behavior with a new unneurotic pattern. Psychotherapy does not merely add new information to our psyches, it replaces or corrects misinformation which was decreasing our ability to predict and control. A racially prejudiced person is, by definition, neurotic, since he incorporates misleading information. If through education he learns to accept persons on the basis of their individual merit, he has undergone psychotherapy, either formally or informally. He will, as a consequence, be better able to predict and control his environment.

The preceding tells us what psychotherapy is supposed to be and what many of its practitioners, including Ethical Therapists, in one way or another, claim it is. However, as we examine the history of psychotherapy, we will see that it has consisted mainly of psychofraud.

Ancient History

Psychotherapy is probably as old as man, since in a simple sense it involves replacing bad habits with good habits. Aristotle, for example, had the preceding view of treating mental illness. Any parent who tried to eliminate bad habits and teach good ones to his children was, in a sense, practicing psychotherapy. The criteria of what is "good" and what is "bad," of course, vary from place to place and time to time. The only common denominator seems to be that activities which increase our ability to predict and control are generally considered "good" and activities which diminish it are generally considered "bad." Even when we look in retrospect at what we know were bad activities, such as the burning of heretics by the Inquisition, we can see that the leaders of the Church actually thought that they were increasing the collective ability of mankind to predict and control.

The hierarchy of the Church thought that the most important part of the environment was the soul. The most important thing to predict and control was whether the soul went to heaven or hell when we died. Their prediction was that the souls of heretics all went to hell and that through their evil influence the heretics could drag others to hell with them. Therefore, they exercised control over their environment by burning the heretics so that they would not decrease the ability of the faithful to predict and control the future lives of their souls. From the point of view of the Church hierarchy, the Inquisition was good and increased the collective ability to predict and control. Burning heretics was a type of public psychotherapy. The evil the Church did resulted not from bad intentions, but from psychofraud.*

Psychofraud becomes highly destructive and reaches the malignant proportions of the Inquisition when it becomes incorporated as a tenet of a political system. In our own day this destructive psychofraud occurred in Nazi Germany and Soviet Russia, where the leaders used tactics by which even the Inquisition pales—all in an effort to increase their ability to predict and control.

Throughout human history psychotherapy has been practiced not so much by professional therapists and ideologues as by parents in raising their children. Parents intuitively have used conditioning techniques of psychotherapy by punishing their children when they were "bad" and rewarding them when they were "good." Long before Pavlov, Watson, and Skinner advocated conditioning techniques for

* It should be noted that when the Protestants had political power, they were just as zealous in burning heretics as were the Catholics. No one has ever had a monopoly on psychofraud.

shaping behavior, parents used these techniques to eliminate "bad" habits and create "good" habits in their children.* Furthermore, these techniques of control worked; otherwise human evolution could not have continued (50).

Although this informal family-based type of psychotherapy is the one most extensively used and by all accounts the most successful, it is largely ignored by professional psychotherapists except in its negative aspects. That family-based conditioning therapy can have deleterious effects is evidenced by the existence of highly neurotic adults whose anxieties and emotions prevent them from predicting and controlling their environment at anywhere near their organic potential. Some of these neurotic adults are produced by neurotic parents who conditioned them to accept "bad" habits as "good" and "good" habits as "bad." This is one way in which neuroses can be inherited nongenetically.

From now on we will call a habit, i.e., behavior pattern, "good" if and only if it increases our ability to predict and control the total environment. Similarly, we call a habit "bad" if and only if it decreases our ability to predict and control the total environment. That most persons throughout history have learned more good than bad habits is evidenced by the fact that the collective ability of the human race to predict and control its total environment has steadily increased for thousands of years and has increased spectacularly in the last three hundred years. This is evidenced not only by our increase in numbers, which is the main objective biological criterion for the success of a species, but also by our ability to predict and control our physical environment, ranging from eclipses and weather to space travel and nuclear energy.

* It should be noted that behaviorists have made a very valuable contribution to psychosocial science by showing that rewarding desirable behavior is a more effective way of shaping behavior than by punishing undesirable behavior.

Today we better predict and control our biological environment through scientific agriculture and by understanding the causes of disease, thereby developing inoculation techniques, antibiotics and even genetic engineering. In the physical and biological environment, our ability to predict and control has grown spectacularly. This is obviously the case, even if we are on the brink of self-destruction through nuclear and ecological disaster. These disasters are imminent not because we cannot predict and control the physical and biological environment adequately, but because we cannot predict and control ourselves.

Predicting and Controlling Behavior

To predict and control the psychosocial environment is to be able to predict and control human behavior, including our own. It is the purpose of social "science" in general and psychotherapy in particular to do this. In accordance with our criteria of "good" and "bad," what we wish to do is to increase creative behavior and decrease destructive behavior.

To be creative is to organize the environment into new patterns which increase the net ability of the human race to predict and control the total environment. If we have done no more than increased our own ability and not decreased anyone else's ability, then we have been creative. The more creative we are, the more we increase the ability of others and ourselves to predict and control.

To be destructive, on the other hand, is to decrease the ability of others and ourselves to predict and control. To cause physical injury to a human being is destructive because it decreases his ability to predict and control, as was shown in the section on health. To teach a human being something new and true is to be creative, because we have then organized part of the environment, i.e., the person's mind, into a new pattern which increases his ability to predict and control. Creativity is the highest form of intelligence.

Traditionally, psychotherapy has put its emphasis on

increasing a person's ability to predict and control his own emotions. It was not so much creative ability that psychotherapy sought to increase, as the elimination of destructive emotion. The reason for this was pragmatic. Persons did not usually go to a psychotherapist to learn how to better build bridges, perform higher mathematics, breed animals, avoid infectious disease, paint pictures or compose symphonies (28, 29, 43, 71, 146). If they were interested in these subjects, they went to an expert in the particular subject. However, if they found they were so full of anxiety that they could not create or even perform routine functions, they saw a psychotherapist (43, 71). If they were so overcome with jealousy, hate or fear that they could not concentrate on their studies or work, they saw a psychotherapist (43, 71). If they were so depressed that death seemed a better alternative than life, they saw a psychotherapist. Psychotherapy, therefore, developed as a technique for dealing with the immediate problems of neurotics and not as a technique for making persons creative. Although some therapies claim to increase creativity, there is no objective evidence that they actually do so (6, 7, 38, 91, 147, 148, 172, 183).

Religion and Therapy

The early professional therapists were almost all religious priests of some kind. When a devout Catholic unburdens his soul to his confessor, he is assured that the slate has been wiped clear and he need feel no more anxiety or guilt after doing proper penance. This is analogous to the highly effective psychofraud of selling one's warts to another. For a devout Catholic, his religion in general and confession in particular take care of all important mental problems. Once he has confessed, he is assured of eternal bliss in heaven, if he should die before having committed new "mortal sins."

This is powerful medicine. It is psychofraud. It may eliminate anxiety, but there is no evidence that it increases creativity. Indeed, it may decrease creativity by deluding the believer into thinking that all important questions are answered and that he need not achieve in this world but merely prepare himself for the really good life in the next. It is probably more than a coincidence that the most creative regions in Europe before the Reformation, Italy and Iberia (Spain and Portugal), remained the most Catholic afterward and have undergone a drastic decrease in creativity since then relative to the Protestant countries of Northern Europe. Between Catholic Ireland and Protestant Scotland, we see a similar contrast in creativity under more controlled conditions. Therefore, even when conventional psychotherapy accomplishes its stated purpose of relieving destructive emotion, it is not necessarily a good thing, if it does not increase and, in fact, decreases creativity.

Modern psychotherapy developed as a secular alternative to Catholic confession. Modern psychotherapy was developed mainly by Jews, e.g., Freud, Adler, Rank, Reich, Perls, Fromm, and Maslow, and to a much lesser extent Protestants, e.g., Jung and Rogers. Catholics, perhaps because of their low creativity, but most of all because they already had a highly effective form of psychofraud, did not participate to any notable extent in the creation of modern psychotherapy. It should be noted that Freud and his circle were mostly Jews living in a largely Catholic country. Jung was the son of a Protestant minister. In our own time, the highly popular psychotherapist, Rollo May, was originally trained as a Protestant minister. The connection between psychotherapy and religion is very close (29, 54, 84, 88, 165). The psychiatrist, E. F. Torrey, in his 1972 book, *The Mind Game*, quite candidly admits that witch doctors and psychotherapists use many of the same techniques and are effective for similar reasons. However, he sees this as indicative of the value of witch doctors and not of the disvalue of psychotherapists.

The effectiveness of the Catholic religion in relieving emotional stress is objectively evidenced by the much lower rate of suicide and demand for psychotherapy in most Catholic countries (40, 44, 87, 178). The ratio is about twenty to one in favor of the Catholic countries. For the most part, it is the "fallen" Catholics who seem to feel great emotional stress until they find some new kind of psychofraud. In European communist countries, where the political ideology preempts all other forms of psychofraud, the therapeutic confession is almost totally lacking, and the suicide rates are climbing dramatically. Hungary, a traditionally Catholic country now under communist control, now has the highest rate in the world (178).

Virtually all persons (over 90 percent) who undergo psychotherapy claim it brings them emotional relief and that it has enabled them to better cope with life (42, 43, 91, 146). It makes little difference whether the therapy is Roman Catholic, Freudian, Christian Science, Adlerian, Jungian, Rogerian, Reichian, "humanistic" or "dianetic"—the results seem to be about the same (42, 43). Anxiety is reduced and creativity is at best unaffected; at worst it may be decreased, as was shown to be the case for Roman Catholic therapy and has been repeatedly documented (24, 148, 152, 153, 154, 183).

With the exception of behavior therapy, which is a modern version of the age-old custom of psychological conditioning, modern systems of psychotherapy have no significant objective criteria for measuring their effectiveness. The expressed subjective feelings of the patient are considered the best indication of the success of the treatment. Behavior therapy is different from most of the modern forms of psychotherapy in its aim and in its effects. It will be discussed separately.

From now on, when we refer to modern psychotherapy, we refer to all systems other than behavior therapy and Ethical Therapy. It will be shown that both Ethical and Behavior Therapy share a certain objectivity and scientific approach with each other but not with other forms of modern therapy. They differ in that behavior therapy is symptom oriented and does not increase or even seek to increase creativity, while Ethical Therapy is oriented entirely toward increasing the total creativity of the person.

RATIONALISTIC THERAPY

All modern forms of psychotherapy are derived from the teachings of Freud. They assume that there are unconscious processes operating in human beings and that most neurotic behavior is a response to unconscious desires and needs. Depending on the system in question, it is assumed that all behavior is learned except for certain innate drives or needs.

Freudianism

Freud thought that there were only two innate needs, the life drive (eros) and the death wish (thanathos). The life drive manifested itself in our sexual desires, love, and our instinct for self-preservation. The death wish manifested itself in all our destructive behavior, e.g., aggression and suicide. Freud's therapy, psychoanalysis, consisted in helping the patient become aware of his basic unconscious needs, which had been repressed by certain unconscious mechanisms of the mind, which found these primal needs unacceptable. According to Freud, the primary source of mental illness stemmed from improper sexual development, particularly the Oedipus complex, by means of which children repressed their sexual desires for their parents. Freud thought the Oedipus complex universal. Once the mechanisms by which the patient repressed his basic thoughts became clear to the patient through insight, the patient's neuroses vanished. It is to the credit of Freud that at the core of his therapy was the belief that "the truth will make you free." The problem stemmed from his lack of scientific rigor and the acceptance of subjective truth in lieu of objective truth.* Ethical Therapy is based entirely

* The differences between subjective and objective truth are discussed in Part Two.

on objective truth. There is no scientific evidence whatever that psychoanalysis, as a theory, has any validity other than in its basic assumption about the existence of unconscious states. In other words, it simply does not seem to work except as a placebo (33, 38, 48, 73, 91, 116, 123, 148, 152, 183). These and hundreds of controlled experiments in which psychoanalyzed patients were compared to various control groups show that psychoanalysis is of little or no *medical* value, although the psychotherapeutic confession, which can occur independently of psychoanalytic theory, may have some nonspecific *emotional* value.

Adlerism

Alfred Adler, a student and colleague of Freud, believed that there was only one basic need, the will-to-power. All of human activity was seen as a means of acquiring power. When the drive to power is thwarted by environmental forces beyond one's control, then neuroses set in. These manifest themselves in ways of deceiving one's self about one's own dependency or impotence, e.g., an inferiority complex. However, Adler saw a healthy person using his power to help his fellowmen in open friendship and not exploiting them. The willful domination of one person by another was seen as a form of neurosis and as a compensation for feelings of inferiority. Adlerian psychotherapy, *individual psychology*, consisted in helping persons recognize their own basic need for power and channelling it into creative activity as well as recognizing the mechanisms which were used to compensate for feelings for inferiority. The scientific validity of Adlerism is at the same stage as Freudianism. However, because Adler assumed less than Freud, he had less about which he could be wrong. All things being equal, simple models are preferable to more complex models.

Reichianism

Wilhelm Reich, another pupil of Freud, thought that the basis of all neuroses resulted from the inability to achieve full orgasm. There was a substance in the universe called "orgone energy" which a person tapped when he had a good orgasm or sat in a special box Reich invented called an "orgone accumulator." Orgone therapy consisted mostly in sitting in the orgone accumulator and then having a good orgasm. Patients who did not have a sexual partner were encouraged to masturbate—the reverse of the old masturbatory hypothesis. Reich claimed that orgone therapy not only cured neuroses but virtually every other disease as well, including cancer. He claimed that he could even create life within his orgone accumulators, i.e., synthesize protozoa from matter and energy. Furthermore, he documented all his results with sufficient detail so that anyone who wished it could duplicate his "experiments." Although his theories are among the most fantastic, they are also among the most scientific in claiming a controlled experimental basis. The fact that Reich's experiments have never been duplicated by any independent scientist makes it highly likely that orgone therapy is also psychofraud.

Although orgone therapy may be psychofraud, it is a most effective placebo. Many faithful adherents of orgone treatment claim wonders for it, even after all other forms of psychotherapy and medical treatment had failed (112). There is a growing cult of true believers around Reich's Orgone Institute even as Freud's, Adler's, and the other rationalistic therapists' orthodox followers diminish (112). Reich himself is widely considered to have been insane by the more orthodox therapists. Objectively, he seems at least as successful as his rivals in predicting and controlling human behavior in terms of his documented cures and the dedication of his followers.

Reich, Adler, and Freud, as well as many other schools of psychotherapy derived from Freudianism, share a common rationalistic approach. This rationalism appeals to the nonmystical, but it is unscientific, because the theories are not based on objectively verifiable experiments. The experiments that Reich did were apparently elaborate forms of self deception. Furthermore, Reich's theory made many predictions about purely physical facts which are untrue, e.g., he claimed that the blueness of the oceans and the skies was due to orgone energy and not to light diffraction. This can easily be shown to be false. Still Reich's psychofraud is among the most effective placebos because it has an aura of magic and complex mechanistic science about it, which the more traditional forms of psychotherapy lack. It is the magical ingredient which makes psychofraud most effective (42, 43). It is the synthesis between psychotherapy and mysticism which is growing and threatens to destroy Western Civilization, even as it destroyed the great civilizations of the East.

MYSTICAL THERAPY

Mystical therapy differs from rationalistic therapy in calling into play alleged supernatural powers with which to produce its effects. Faith healers, who claim to have special powers given to them by an all-powerful god or gods, range from witch doctors to Christian ministers. When persons believe the faith healer, the placebo effect of this belief is overwhelming and can overshadow any pseudoscientific placebo, such as sugar pills, orgone boxes or psychoanalysis. For this reason witch doctors can kill their enemies with sympathetic magic. For this reason the blind can be made to see and the cripple to walk. When the faith healing cannot overcome a completely organic disorder, such as missing organs or limbs, the faith healer need only say that the patient was not cured because of his lack of faith, that if he had truly believed he would have been cured.

Christian Science

The first modern attempt to bring about a synthesis between therapy and mysticism was made by Mary Baker

Eddy in the nineteenth century, when she founded Christian Science. Mark Twain referred to her as "the most remarkable woman who ever lived." As an organizational genius she has had few peers. She puts Freud and all his intellectual descendants to shame.

Mary Baker was born to rigid Calvinists in 1821. She was a sickly girl, but she managed to acquire three husbands during her lifetime. She apparently suffered from a wide variety of psychosomatic and hysterical diseases. Her second husband, Dr. Patterson, a dentist, after being unsuccessful in curing her symptoms, sent her to a famous Mesmerist, Phineas Quimby, who had combined hypnotic suggestion with primitive Christian faith healing. He apparently had a profound effect on the then Mrs. Mary Baker Glover Patterson. After a few sessions with Quimby, she is reputed to have glowed with health for the first time in her life.

She had for many years been attracted to mysticism, occultism and spiritualism. After her experience with Quimby, she was certain that she had found ultimate truth. She out-Quimbied Quimby and denied the effects of suggestion and hypnosis. Indeed, with almost uncanny clairvoyance, she preceded modern physics by denying the existence of matter altogether. Mind was the ultimate reality, and matter was merely an evil manifestation of the mind. Since there was no matter, there was no body. All disease could then be cured by mystical Christian exercises, and cure disease she did.

Probably no form of psychofraud can produce as many "documented" cures as can Christian Science (35). It is unreasonable to assume that Christian Science became a powerful, wealthy, world-wide movement with millions of adherents merely because of wishful thinking. It grew and prospered because it worked. It was one of the most powerful placebos ever created. Its only limitation was that it would not work on persons who were not orthodox Christians. For them another type of mystical placebo with scientific overtones was necessary. It was to be created by Carl Gustav Jung.

Jungianism

Jung had been Freud's favorite associate and his heir apparent. However, Jung's Calvinistic background and mystical nature did not permit him to accept Freud's purely mechanistic concepts of the mind or the importance of the sex "drive" in human development. Jung believed in the "collective unconscious" by means of which the human race shares a common memory. Religious belief and practice was a symbolic expression of collective unconscious knowledge. Freud was antagonistic toward religion, whereas Jung encouraged his patients to practice the religion in which they felt most comfortable. The hierarchy of the Catholic Church was most antagonistic toward Freud but quite friendly toward Jung. Several Catholic priests have been Jungian therapists. For obvious reasons, the Nazis were antagonistic toward Freud, but they embraced Jung as he embraced them.

To Jung the basis of all neuroses lay in unresolved, unconscious conflicts. He saw all persons as basically introverted or extroverted. Furthermore, irrespective of which basic type they were, they could be oriented toward sensation, intuition, feeling or thinking. Each person would emphasize one or another of these ways of being. However, within each person there was another hidden part, "the shadow," which longed to express itself. Therefore, a thinking introvert unconsciously longed to be an intuitive, sensual or feeling extrovert, or some other combination of the eight basic categories of personalities. Furthermore, there were in each person ideas and thoughts which had not yet "ripened" and would eventually have to express themselves.

Psychotherapy consisted in helping the patient recognize this "shadow" self and express these unconscious desires. Sex was merely one of many unconscious desires that a person might have suppressed.

So far, this approach is not too different from Freud. The main difference is on emphasis. Jung also felt that many emotional problems arose from aimlessness and purposelessness in one's life. For this reason religion was encouraged as a means of giving purpose to existence. What is unique to Jung and those he has influenced is the concept of the "collective unconscious."

The notion of a collective unconscious can exist without any mystical assumptions. For example, we merely note that all memories correspond to some physical state in the brain and that some initial memories, i.e., brain states, are synthesized by the genes. However, the Jungians seem to feel, in a rather nebulous way, that the experiences of each person somehow affect the unconscious memories of all persons, and that some of these memories are inherited in a way that is neither Lamarkian or Darwinian.* This is the mystical part of Jung which makes the mind more akin to a soul and sets the ground for the immortality of the ego as a possibility.

For this reason Jungian analysis, which is called *analytic psychology*, is very appealing to religious and mystical persons. Older persons who begin to be concerned about death also find considerable comfort in Jung's theories. Artists and creative persons in general are attracted by the possibility of increasing their creativity through (1) helping their "unripened ideas" emerge from their unconscious and

* Lamarkianism, also called Michurinism and Lysenkoism, assumes that acquired characteristics, such as a sunburned skin, are passed on by heredity from parent to child. Darwinism assumes that only physical changes in the genes influence heredity and that any gross changes in the body of a parent will not be inherited. All scientific evidence supports Darwinism.

(2) tapping the collective unconscious which is alleged to be the major source of creativity. Analytic psychology claims to facilitate this process. There is absolutely no scientific evidence that any theories peculiar to Jung are valid (33, 38, 48, 73, 91, 113, 116, 123, 148, 152, 183).

THE REVOLT AGAINST REASON

The spirit of rationalism which manifested itself in logical positivism and dialectic materialism during the first half of the twentieth century was unfavorable to Jung. Freud fared much better, although he was just as unscientific as Jung and less imaginative. However, the "revolt against reason" which has been an undercurrent in human thought since the time of Rousseau, has gathered new strength in recent years.

This strength comes mainly from the reaction to modern science and its manifestations in the materialistic civilization of the United States, Western Europe and the Soviet Bloc. These societies, which claim to have embraced modern science, have produced a new generation of alienated, affluent youth who seek spiritual values. They see "heroic materialism" leading the world toward human degradation, pollution and annihilation. Therefore, they reject reason, which they sometimes call "linear thinking," and, above all, science as a means to a better life. Among the post-atomic generation, primitive Christianity, Hare Krishna, Jungianism and other forms of mystical therapy are in great vogue. However, the leading edge of this movement is represented by *humanistic psychology.*

Humanistic Psychology

Humanistic psychology is the culmination of all types of psychofraud. It might be called "eclectic psychofraud." All the forces of mysticism, scientism and anti-scientific thinking have come together under a single militant banner. The central belief of the humanistic psychologists is that ultimate reality is subjective, not objective. It is our thoughts and emotions that count, not whether these thoughts and emotions lead to any objectively verifiable ability to predict and control the external environment. The emphasis is on doing one's own thing and accepting any behavior, no matter how bizarre, as normal and natural. Indeed, the more peculiar and entertaining the behavior, the more liberated the person is. The only ethical constraints are "be happy" and "do not make others unhappy" (179).

The "scientific" basis of humanistic psychology is found in the writings of Abraham Maslow. Maslow believed that human beings were born with a biologically predetermined hierarchy of needs. If "lower" needs were left "unsatisfied," "higher" needs would not manifest themselves. Briefly, the major classes of needs in the hierarchy are as follows: (1) security (includes basic instincts of self-preservation and hunger), (2) love (includes the sex drive, affection, kindness, altruism, etc.), (3) self-esteem (includes being highly regarded by one's self and others), and (4) self-actualization (includes the need to be free, creative and self-directing).

Any creative scientist or artist may be self-actualizing. However, persons such as Stalin and Hitler also fall into the self-actualizing category. Each did his own thing. They displayed considerable imagination and resourcefulness in accomplishing tasks they set for themselves. They did not merely cater to other persons' expectations and seek to please. Therefore, a person may be self-actualizing and still highly neurotic, by our definition. However, in Maslow's scheme neuroses stem from having unfulfilled lower needs which prevent a person from becoming self-actualizing. Once a person has become self-actualizing, he is considered "healthy."

In all fairness to Maslow it should be pointed out that he was much more rational and hardheaded than those who have incorporated his teachings into humanistic psychology. He was unscientific but not antiscientific. He was very much in the tradition of the speculative, rationalistic psychotherapists, such as Freud, Adler, and the Gestalt therapists. However, there is no scientific evidence to support Maslow's theories. Their uncritical acceptance by the humanistic psychologists brings them into the realm of psychofraud, even if some of these theories, such as the quite plausible hierarchy of needs, should later be shown to be partially true.

Therapy in humanistic psychology consists in helping persons recognize and fulfill their alleged basic needs. If a person is lacking love, he will be at a fairly primitive level of development. Therefore, a humanistic psychotherapist should help the patient recognize and fulfill his needs for love.

Some humanistic psychologists treat their patients through sexual intercourse, thereby satisfying the patient's need for "love." Most of the therapists who practice this type of sex therapy are heterosexual males. However, there have been reports of this "therapy" applied to persons of both sexes by the "therapist" (24, 132). A few female therapists also claim to practice it selectively (132). There is one report of a massive group sex-therapy session where many sex therapists and their patients had a party and engaged in "patient swapping" (132). The sex therapists have not clarified whether they use sexual intercourse as a form of therapy for all their sexually deprived patients or only for those they find attractive. However, sex therapy is one of the more banal variants of humanistic psychology.

Paul Bindrim, the originator of "nude-marathon group therapy," where neurotics sit nude in a group, "interact," and discuss their problems for long periods of time, announced a dramatic "breakthrough" in psychotherapy which was highly praised by Maslow himself shortly before his death. Maslow claimed that after exposure to a nude therapy group, "people would go away more spontaneous, less guarded, less defensive, not only about the shape of their behinds, but freer and more innocent about their minds too" (74). Bindrim theorized that the major focus of anatomical anxiety centered around the crotch. If persons could rid themselves of crotch anxiety, they might be able to take a giant step toward mental health and self-actualization. Therefore, he has modified his "nude therapy" into "crotch therapy" (74).

In crotch therapy all the members of the nude-marathon therapy group are successively spread-eagled before all the other members who then proceed to stare at the patient's crotch until their and the patient's crotch anxiety is "extinguished," in the parlance of the behaviorists. In extinguishing their crotch anxiety, presumably their other anxieties will also be extinguished. After all of the patients have stared for prolonged periods at each others crotches, according to Bindrim, they report an enormous psychic "boost."

Humanistic psychology has recently become respectable and is now classified as "the thirty-second area of psychology" (179).

The following excerpt of items from *The Whole-Soul Catalogue of Humanistic Psychology* will give a flavor of the sorts of things humanistic psychologists value.

Acid
Aikido
Astrology
Bio-Energetics
Bio-Feedback Devices
Chanting
Dreams
Fasting
Gay Liberation
Group Basic Encounter
Hare Krishna
Human-Potential Expanders
I Ching
International Transcendental-Meditation Society
Meditation
Natural Foods
Nude Research
Open Encounter
Optokinetic Perceptual Learning Device
Paranormal Research
Parapsychology
Psychodrama
Psychosynthesis
Subud
The Tarot
Tibetan Buddhism
Transpersonal Association
Witchcraft

Jesus People	Yoga
Massage	Zen

Humanistic psychology incorporates every conceivable form of psychofraud. In many ways it seeks to make psychotic behavior, as defined here, the norm. The current work of J. C. Lilly bears this out (83).* Therefore, it seems inevitable that humanistic psychology will, in time, preempt all other forms of psychofraud. In so doing, it will have the same effects that psychofraud has had through the ages—it will make people happy. But will it increase creativity?

EFFECTIVENESS OF PSYCHOTHERAPY

The effectiveness of psychofraud in giving people peace of mind, emotional tranquility, and relief from physical and psychoneurotic illness has been amply demonstrated by thousands of case histories and even a few controlled experiments (6, 7, 38, 73, 91, 147, 148, 172, 183). What seems to have been missed by most exponents of psychofraud is that its effectiveness depends mainly on the faith of the patient and is independent of the theory on which it is based.

An experiment showed that psychotherapists of different schools eventually ended by giving identical treatments to all their patients (91). An analysis of their conversations with their patients showed that shortly after finishing their psychotherapeutic training they used language and took an approach which was characteristic of their schools, Freudian, Jungian, Adlerian, Gestalt, etc. However, after they had been in practice for several years there seemed to be no discernable difference between the treatment given by the therapists from the different schools (42, 43). Furthermore, they seemed to have become more effective therapists with

* See excerpt about humanistic psychology given on pages 32 and 33.

time. What is the explanation?

The only explanations which make sense in this context are the following: (1) merely talking over one's problems with intelligent, sympathetic listeners with whom one is not too emotionally involved is occasionally an effective form of therapy for some nonbiological illnesses; (2) a person can become a better listener and more effective therapist with practice; and (3) believing that some experience will cure and control anxiety is enough to make it work. In other words, almost all the years spent in learning various theories explaining psychotic and neurotic behavior and how to treat it are irrelevant. What counts is merely being a good listener and exuding confidence. The more confidence he exudes the more effective a placebo the therapist becomes. The patient is treated by psychofraud; but the major victim of psychofraud has been the therapist, who, with the best of intentions, has wasted a large portion of his life learning useless theories.

In 1973 a Ph.D. candidate in counselling and psychotherapy did a well-controlled experiment as part of her doctoral dissertation, to evaluate the relative effectiveness of short-term and long-term eclectic psychotherapy. With considerable difficulty she was persuaded to include in her study a control group which would not be given any kind of treatment. The experimental and control subjects were all students from the same school who had sought psychotherapeutic help at the university counselling center. The students were assigned randomly to three groups: short term (I), long term (II) and control (III). The control group was merely placed on the waiting list and was not treated, although for experimental purposes this was a type of "treatment." All the students were given batteries of validated, standardized psychological tests to determine their mental health before and after treatment. It was discovered after treatment that there were no significant differences between the psychological states of the three groups as measured by any of the objective tests. In this case there was not even a discernible placebo effect. Any psychological changes were due to time, biology and external causes.

This is not too surprising in view of the preceding discussions. What was surprising was the response of the experimenter who could not believe her own experimental data and tried desperately to find a psychotherapeutic effect when there was none. She could not accept the fact that after spending four hard years in studying to be a psychotherapist she had learned little more than psychofraud. However, her experiment was well conceived and performed, and she was awarded the Ph.D. She now is teaching the same psychofraud which her own experiment showed to be ineffective at a large university. She continues to see patients and to practice psychofraud (175).

The lesson to be drawn from this example is that the victims of psychofraud find it difficult to face reality even when it comes from direct personal experience. The emotional and sometimes financial investment made in psychofraud blinds its victims to reality. Thousands of similar, well-controlled experiments have been done which expose psychofraud for what it is; yet its practitioners and victims remain true believers. They will grasp at any straw which supports their belief and reject a mountain of evidence which contradicts it.

Part of the problem is that there are thousands of case histories and poorly controlled experiments which tend to support the position of conventional psychotherapy. Any time a person undergoing psychotherapy shows improvement, it is assumed to be due to the treatment and not to any external or biological causes. Unsuccessful cases are usually ignored. Any positive evidence is uncritically accepted and the hard negative evidence is categorically rejected. The need to believe comforting illusions is often greater than the need for objective truth.

When psychotherapists claim that there is evidence both ways regarding psychotherapy, i.e., (1) evidence tending to support the validity of psychotherapy and (2) evidence tending to contradict it, they are really saying in effect that the well-controlled experiments tend to contradict the claims of psychotherapy and the poorly controlled experiments tend to support it. It is relatively easy to do well-controlled experiments; yet they are rarely done in psychotherapy or in any branch of social "science," for that matter. The investment in the established social science ideologies is too great. The question remaining is, Are there any benefits to be derived from a formal study of any of the conventional forms of psychotherapy?

It may be argued that if the therapist had not gone through the ritual of studying psychofraud in a formal setting, he would not have had enough confidence or credentials to be an effective placebo to his patient. However, we know through thousands of documented cases that many faith healers and hypnotists seem to achieve results as good as or better than some certified psychotherapists (23, 59, 62, 73, 91, 92, 95). Therefore, what is real and sometimes works in psychotherapy is suggestion and catharsis through conversation and other forms of communication (42, 43). It matters not so much how the patient has come to believe that he can understand, control and predict his psychic environment as that he in fact does believe. This will occasionally eliminate emotional problems, but it will not necessarily make persons more creative.

A survey of the literature and the current state of affairs leads one to suspect that there are four, and only four elements of value in psychotherapy. These are as follows:

1. Discussing one's problems with intelligent, sympathetic listeners, irrespective of their psychotherapeutic training, fulfills some basic human needs. This can relieve anxiety and help persons see themselves in a more rational framework. People need friends, even paid friends.
2. Suggestion, whether through placebos or hypnosis,

can alter a person's mental and physical state. A self-confident psychotherapist with impressive (to the patient) credentials can be a most effective placebo or hypnotist. The patient might be more prone to suggestion from him than from a "layman."

3. Conditioning, Pavlovian and operant, can change simple behavior and cure simple neuroses such as phobias and compulsions. This is extensively discussed in the next chapter.

4. Learning how to cope scientifically with as much of the physical, biological, and psychosocial environment as possible in an integrated way can relieve anxiety and reduce neuroses. This approach is discussed at length in Part Two and is an integral part of Ethical Therapy.

The rationalistic school of psychiatry led by J. D. Frank at Johns Hopkins has independently reached similar conclusions, as have other therapists (42, 43).

Of course, drugs and surgery can also modify behavior. But we have by definition excluded these approaches from psychotherapy, although they can be part of ethical medical treatment.

Some forms of psychofraud, such as religion and humanistic psychology, are so much out of tune with reality that although they provide enormous emotional comfort, they delude persons into believing that all aspects of nature can be controlled by the same type of magic. Persons so convinced will eventually succumb to such nonpsychic phenomena as bacterial or viral infections, crop failures, floods, earthquakes and other natural disasters, which they have tried to control through purely magical means, such as prayer or "transcendental meditation." Although most modern forms of psychotherapy do not pretend to have any relevance outside of human emotions and behavior, some, such as Christian Science, orgonomy and humanistic psychology, have been extrapolated to explain many forms of natural phenomena. Christian Science denies the existence of the material universe altogether. Orgone theory explains the blueness of nature and the origins of life. It claims to cure cancer. Humanistic psychology explains many forms of complex social behavior, such as war, in terms of its form of psychofraud. It induces persons to believe that drug-generated psychotic states or self-delusion represent a higher reality (83, 179). It induces persons into accepting food fads and astrology as means of predicting and controlling their biological and physical environment. It makes them reject scientific method as a means of copying with reality.

The antiscientific aspect of psychofraud in general and humanistic psychology in particular is the most pernicious. The rejection of scientific method bodes almost certain disaster for the human race. This is the case because the most serious human problems arise from having created a world in which science and technology have radically altered the physical and biological environment while the psychosocial environment is still controlled by psychofraud. It will not be until the same criteria of objective verifiability are used to determine the truth or falsity of psychosocial theories that the total environment will again be brought into proper balance. This is the purpose of Ethical Therapy. It is also the *stated* purpose of behaviorism.

4

Behaviorism

> *To the very last days of his life, every time that Ivan Petrovich Pavlov saw a dog salivate, he would ring a bell.*
>
> Anonymous

Behaviorism is the most scientific kind of psychofraud. It is based on the premise that the purpose of behavioral science is to predict and control human behavior. So far so good. However, it takes as its second premise that all human behavior can be understood, i.e., predicted and controlled, solely by objectively observing human behavior. In other words, according to behaviorism, by merely observing which train of behavioral events ended in a particular type of behavior, we can infer that the same train of events would end in identical behavior for another organism of the same species. There is considerable evidence that this is often, *but not always,* true for many kinds of lower animals; e.g., it is very easy to predict and control maze-running behavior in rats using this approach. There is also evidence that the behavioristic model holds for many types of simple human behavior. More often than not, we can correctly predict human reactions to a strong electrical shock using only past observations to construct a behavioral model. However, behaviorism has never shown that it can significantly enhance human creativity. Behaviorism denies the existence of subjective behavior such as thinking. Since private thought processes are not objectively observable, they are to be denied, as is the existence of the concept of "mind."

MIND

The greatest stumbling block for most persons in accepting behaviorism is in rejecting the existence of their own minds. For if a person knows anything, surely it is that he has a mind. Everything else, including his body and the physical universe may be an illusion, but he cannot be a figment of his own imagination.

The only thing we know with certainty is that we have thoughts and perceptions. We may not be certain what is causing these thoughts and perceptions, but we cannot logically deny to ourselves that we have them. This set of private thoughts and perceptions is what we call our "mind."

Insofar as the mind can predict and control its own thoughts, we say the mind is "conscious." Insofar as the mind has unpredictable and uncontrollable thoughts, we say the mind is "unconscious." Every human being has experienced both conscious and unconscious thoughts; the former, in his deliberate and purposeful behavior; the latter, in dreams and in his uncontrollable emotions, whose origins and fundamental causes he does not grasp. Post-hypnotic thoughts and actions are scientifically verifiable examples of unconscious processes (59, 95). We can alter all our thoughts by altering our brain (13, 139, 140). Physical, chemical and electrical changes in the brain can change our memories, perceptions and any other mental phenomena (11, 13, 139, 140). These changes can be scientifically replicated and verified in each person. Therefore, the mind is a controllable effect of the body, just as gravity is a controllable effect of matter.

The behaviorists deny the existence of all these aspects of mind, which are clearly and irrefutably self-evident. They feel that by denying the existence of subjective behavior, they are being "scientific purists."

SCIENCE

The behaviorist position in denying the existence of purely subjective mental phenomena consists of the argument paraphrased here:

> We are only concerned with predicting and controlling human behavior. Subjective mental states are not objectively verifiable; only behavior is objectively verifiable. Assumptions about unobservable mental states represent unnecessary hypotheses which contaminate and unnecessarily complicate the behavioral data, which is the only data with which we are concerned. Therefore, we should eliminate all nonbehavioral assumptions and subjective observations, if we are to develop a true science of behavior.

This basic behavioral position was taken by J. B. Watson (163, 164) and his followers—most notable among them, B. F. Skinner (137, 138)—as a means of combatting the psychofraud of the Freudians and the psychotherapists who based their theories on unobservable mental states and mechanisms. It was a sincere desire to develop a true science of the psychosocial environment. However, by denying the obvious existence of mind and subjective behavior, the behaviorists have created a new type of psychofraud.

What distinguishes psychofraud from science is not the objectivity of the input data, but rather the verifiability of the predictions of the models. Psychoanalysis is not psychofraud because it is based on a theory about unobservable mental states. It is psychofraud because its claims at predicting and controlling human behavior cannot be verified scientifically. In controlled experiments, psychoanalysis is no more effective than placebos or other forms of suggestion and in some cases less effective (38, 91, 183). The theory of psychoanalysis has nothing to do with the reasons it works. Christian Science and orgonomy work just as well; and in certain documented cases, both have been shown to work much better (35, 112).

Orgonomy is completely objective in most of its assumptions. Orgone is supposed to be a physically measurable quantity. The fact that no one outside of Reich's followers has ever measured it is not as important as the fact that no controlled experiment has ever shown orgone treatment to be anything other than a placebo effect.

The crux of the problem is the fact that the overwhelming majority of behaviorists and all of its leading exponents, including Watson and Skinner, were, and still are, scientific illiterates. They have no understanding of the deeper aspects of modern science, but only of its outer manifestations. They wish to use the methods of natural science; yet they have never had a systematic knowledge of mathematics, physical science or biology. They are like the cargo cultists of the South Seas who still think in terms of sympathetic magic.

The cargo cultists see an abundance of valuable goods coming out of the holds of ships and airplanes. They think that there is something intrinsic in the form of these objects which makes them produce like a horn of plenty. They build crude models of ships and planes in the hope that they will produce goods for them. They have no concept of the goods being manufactured in factories and then shipped thousands of miles by these devices.

The scientifically illiterate behaviorists saw that physical science models were based on objectively measurable data. They also saw that the physical sciences were highly effective in predicting the physical environment. Like the cargo cultists, they simulated the outward forms of physical science but missed its deeper significance.

The success of modern science rests not on objective measurement but on objective verification of its predictions. The Ptolomeic model of the earth-centered universe was completely objective. Newton's general theory of gravitation assumed a nonobservable and seemingly mystical entity, "gravity." Gravity had no substance, but it was produced by matter and would affect matter at a distance. Gravity is a physical analogue of mind. Mind has no substance, but it is produced by life and matter and can affect life and matter. The Newtonian model was accepted because it made better predictions than the Ptolomeic model, not because it was more objectively determined.

Pre-Newtonian astronomy was a physical analogue of behaviorism. It merely measured the behavior of celestial bodies and predicted future behavior on the basis of this behavior. It made no assumptions about such mystical concepts as action at a distance. It was not until Newton had the imagination to postulate the concept of a simple, nonpurposive force that man had a scientific alternative to the psychofraud of (1) the universe as a plaything of capricious gods and (2) simple physical behaviorism. The success of this approach is continued in modern science, which postulates all manner of nonobservable entities ranging from force fields to atoms and elementary particles. These postulates are accepted if and only if they improve the ability to predict and control.

In biology the concept of a gene was postulated and used effectively long before there were electron microscopes for observing genes. The gene theory was accepted because it enabled one to predict and control animal and plant breeding. A theory of mind should be accepted if and only if it increases our objectively verifiable ability to predict and control human behavior. To accept any behavioral theory on any other basis is to accept psychofraud.

BEHAVIOR

Human behavior is both objective and subjective. Objective behavior can be observed by *more than one person*. Subjective behavior can only be observed by *one person*, the person behaving. From personal experience we all know that our subjective behavior can affect our objective behavior. For example, when a person does a mental calculation of what the outcome of several possible actions might be and then chooses one particular action based on his calculation, his objective behavior has been modified by his subjective behavior.

A behaviorist would try to predict the final behavior entirely by having observed previous objective behavior. If he had observed every event in the person's life, he might be able to make a good prediction of immediate future behavior. However, in "real life" this is not practical, although it is technically possible. Therefore, the behaviorist will have a very poor model for predicting objective behavior which results from subjective behavior.

Anyone postulating a mental model could estimate a person's subjective mental state by observing a few samples of objective behavior and using his knowledge of his own subjective behavior. If his mental model were a good one, he would make better predictions from the same number of objective observations than a behaviorist possibly could. In our everyday practical actions of predicting and controlling the behavior of other persons, we intuitively assume that other persons are similar to us and will behave similarly. This is based on an introspective model of mental behavior.

There seems to be a one-to-one correspondence between mental states and brain states (13). Mind states should eventually be shown to be objective, just as quantum states can be objectively demonstrated although no one has ever seen a quantum. Personality and intelligence tests are more objective attempts at developing mental models.

PERSONALITY AND INTELLIGENCE

A true behaviorist denies the existence of personality and intelligence, since these are mental states. He would say that how a person acts in the future depends entirely on what has happened to him in the past. Since there is no mind, there are no mental differences, but only different experiences, which result in different behavior. Implied in this is the notion that human beings are identical in innate potential and that they differ behaviorally only because of environmental differences. This denies all the evidence of biology in general and behavioral genetics in particular.

For our purposes we have defined *intelligence* as "a person's ability to predict and control his total environment—physical, biological and psychosocial." We define *personality* as that part of his intelligence which determines (1) what aspects of the environment he will choose to predict and control and (2) to what extent he is resolved to effect this prediction and control. Personality is, therefore, a subset of intelligence, and both are effects of certain body states, e.g., brain and endocrine states (50). We know from elementary biology that the basic structure of our bodies is determined primarily by our genes and not by our environment, although in unusual circumstances, such as surgery, environment can have profound bodily effects.

The preponderance of scientific evidence to date indicates that within a modern, democratic, and at least partially socialized culture, bodily states, and consequently behavior, are primarily, not entirely, determined by heredity (39, 69, 180). Environment can have a profound *differential* effect only on those populations which have been exposed to extreme environmental hardships, such as gross nutritional deficiencies and almost complete denial of educational opportunity. Therefore, differential intelligence is determined almost entirely by differential heredity in any truly democratic society. However, the extreme behaviorists take the opposite view. This view is psychofraud.

The environmental determinism of the behaviorists is expressed quite succinctly in the famous dictum of J. B. Watson, the founding father of behaviorism: "Give me a dozen healthy* infants, well formed, and my own specified world to bring them up in and I guarantee to take any one at random and train him to become any type of specialist I might select—doctor, lawyer, artist, merchant, chief. And, yes, even beggarman and thief, regardless of his talents, penchants, tendencies, abilities, vocations and race of his ancestors."

The current leader of behaviorism, B. F. Skinner, has expressed the same sentiment in many of his writings and public statements (137, 138). On a television show in 1971, when Skinner was asked by the interviewer if he could have painted like Michelangelo if he had been raised in the same environment, Skinner answered a most emphatic, "Yes!"

A simple counter example to the behaviorists' notion that human beings are a *tabula rasa*, upon which the environment prints the story of their lives, occurs in the field of athletics. We all know that in certain fields of athletics we can all learn to improve our performance, but no matter how we practice we cannot begin to match the performance of some outstanding athletes. We can all learn to play baseball, but not many of us can learn to play as well as Babe Ruth or Willie Mays.

A behaviorist might counter this argument by admitting that there are biologically determined differences in athletic

* Watson's concept of "health" was limited to the absence of physical disease and deformities.

behavior, because this behavior is directly dependent on the physical state of the body, which is objectively observable and measurable. However, so-called innate differences in personality and intelligence are denied because these are assumed mental states which cannot be objectively observed or measured. He might deny the proposition that we can all learn to play chess, but not as well as Bobby Fischer.

A nonbehaviorist would then say that these mental states are in one-to-one correspondence with particular brain states which are objectively observable and measurable (13, 34, 139, 140). Since the brain is as much a part of the body as our bones and muscles, genetically determined differences in brain chemistry and structure are responsible for differences in personality and intelligence. Just as we cannot teach a chimpanzee to behave like a normal human being because of a genetically determined difference in brain structure, so we cannot teach a congenital idiot to behave like a genius because of another genetically determined difference in brain structure. At this point the behaviorists would divide themselves into two camps.

In one camp would be the direct-line descendants of Watson, represented by Skinner and his followers. In the other camp would be the philosophical cousins of Watson, such as H. J. Eysenck (38, 39) and A. A. Lazarus (77), who use many of the trappings and methods of behaviorism and sometimes call themselves behaviorists, but recognize that subjective mental states are real or that there are genetically determined differences between persons which cause behavioral differences. The latter, although possibly mistaken in many of their assumptions and analyses, represent the vanguard of scientific psychology and psychotherapy. They are, properly speaking, a subset of Ethical Therapy. They are not, properly speaking, behaviorists. Only Skinnerism is akin to pure behaviorism. Thus, from now on when we refer to behaviorists, we mean only those who practice Skinnerism.

SKINNERISM

No behaviorist, Skinner included, will deny the existence of genetically determined human differences, if confronted directly with the question in a sufficiently clear form. What they do implicitly deny is the importance of these differences, by claiming that any human being can be shaped into whatever any other human being has been shaped. They do not claim that they can shape the behavior of a chimpanzee into that of a normal human being. The behaviorists recognize interspecies genetic differences. They effectively ignore only intraspecies genetic differences. There are three reasons for this: (1) their success in shaping animal behavior so that any healthy animal could be trained to do what any other animal of the same species did; (2) their success in shaping simple noncreative human behavior; and (3) their ignorance of genetics in general and behavioral genetics in particular.

Skinner has trained animals to do the most improbable things, such as teaching pigeons to play ping pong and to control the guidance system of a missile. He has also trained rats to go through very complex behavioral patterns to obtain rewards. Skinner is also an early and effective developer of teaching machines. With human beings, behavior therapists and behavior modifiers (the terms used for behaviorists who treat mental illness or in their term, "deviant behavior") have been very effective in eliminating undesirable habits such as bed wetting, smoking, drinking and, to a lesser extent, sexual deviancy (38, 77, 118, 170, 171). Behavior therapy has also been shown to be highly effective in eliminating phobias, obsessions and compulsions. All in all, there is little doubt that behavioristic techniques can predict and control simple behavior in animals and in humans. What these techniques have *not* been shown to do is to significantly increase creativity.

The basic Skinnerian theory is that all human behavior is determined by operant conditioning. This is a process by which certain behavioral patterns, engaged in at random, are "reinforced." *Reinforcement* is any process which causes the persistence or repetition of a type of behavior and may cause its elimination, if it is not present. For example, giving food to a hungry animal who accidentally presses a lever in a cage will cause the animal to press the lever more and more often every time he gets hungry. Eventually he will unerringly press the lever whenever he wants food. If, after the animal has learned this trick, we cease to give him food every time he presses the lever, he will press it less and less often until he stops pressing altogether, except by chance. This latter process is called "extinction." The giving of the food to the animal is "reinforcement." The lever pressing is the conditioned response. The whole process is an example of operant conditioning.

According to Skinner every conceivable type of behavior in human beings and in animals is brought about by this type of conditioning (137, 138). This includes sex behavior, speech, phobias, aggression, etc. There is no innate predisposition toward any particular kind of behavior. If a certain type of behavior is accompanied by a reward, as in the above example, that behavior will persist. If another type of behavior is accompanied by punishment, such as substituting an electric shock for food in the above example, then that type of behavior will undergo extinction. In this case, the lack of shock is the reinforcement. The removal of the shock itself or other painful experiences is often called "negative reinforcement." The Skinnerians have made an important contribution to human knowledge by showing that positive reinforcement, i.e., rewards, in general are more effective in shaping behavior than negative reinforcement, i.e., punishment. There is considerable evidence that Skinner is correct in his theory except for one critical point, namely, that he claims that there is no significant innate predisposition toward particular kinds of behavior.

What will work as a reinforcer at any given time is determined by the biological structure of the organism *plus* his past experience. For example, a fresh piece of liver will more easily reinforce a hungry cat's behavior than a hungry horse. Similarly, there is considerable scientific evidence (117) that many abnormal types of human behavior ranging from schizophrenia and homosexuality to criminality and alcoholism have genetic causes, in part, but may be mitigated by environmental circumstances. This means that certain environmental factors served as rewards for abnormal persons when they would have been regarded as either neutral or punishment for normal persons. This is analogous to a horse's having a liking for liver. This is one type of genetic difference which Skinner and his followers by and large ignore. They also ignore such things as the biological basis of language (181). More important, however, is their disregard for innate differences in human intellectual potential.

Even if two persons were perfectly normal in their responses to environmental stimuli, they might not have the potential to behave in identical ways any more than a four-foot pygmy has the same innate potential for playing basketball as a seven-foot Watusi, irrespective of the similarity of their training. The Skinnerians, however, claim that they can take any human being at birth and turn him into an Einstein, a Hitler or a Michelangelo solely with operant conditioning. This is psychofraud.

There is absolutely no scientific evidence that operant conditioning alone can turn any person chosen at random into a creative genius or a charismatic leader. For the Skinnerians to insist that they can do this solely because they can teach pigeons to play ping pong, rats to press levers and humans to stop simple neurotic behavior is completely unscientific. One way in which the Skinnerians could scientifically support their claims would be to take a random sample of children at birth from parents of very low ability and train them to be creative geniuses. If they succeeded in producing a significantly higher percentage of creative geniuses among these children than could be expected by chance, the Skinnerians would have a very convincing argument on their side. However, even then they would not have invalidated the possibility of innate differential potential among human beings, since there is a slight possibility that the experimental subjects might have had an enormous environmental advantage.

A definitive experiment for determining the relative effectiveness of genes and environment in producing high intelligence and creativity might take the following simplified form.

Two large groups of mothers would volunteer to put their newborn, well-formed children up for adoption, all to be educated and raised in the best possible behavioristic environment. One group of children would come from mothers of very high intelligence and creativity. Another group of children would come from mothers of very low intelligence and creativity. The children would all be educated by a group of Skinnerians as best they could. This might involve placing each child in a well-to-do foster home or in an idealized behavioristic home environment (137). The experimenters would not know the family background of the children. (This represents a double-blind placebo control.) All children would be given the very best education possible for maximizing their intelligence and creativity. If (1) there were no group differences between the adult performance of the children of the high-ability and low-ability mothers, and (2) both groups performed well above the norm, then the Skinnerians would have been proved correct. Conversely, if there were differences, we could show that genetic differences cause ability differences.

There are more sophisticated experiments for proving or disproving Skinnerian theory which could be done under less drastic conditions. By using elaborate statistical procedures and measures of cosanguinity, we could show the degree of heritability of any kind of behavior. However, this would not convince the Skinnerians, who reject and seem to have little understanding of advanced, modern concepts of statistical control and scientific method.

The most serious criticism that one can level at the Skinnerians is that they, like the rest of the academic community from which they come, are totally oriented toward methods and have no clearly specified ethical end goals or objective criteria for health. They are interested in predicting and controlling behavior as an end in itself. Even if their theory were completely true, they would still have no clear notion about which kind of behavior is "best" for the individual and society. They would have no way of preventing their methods from being used by evil men for evil purposes.

The Skinnerians live in a world of their own with their own language and methods. Like most practitioners of, and believers in, psychofraud, they ignore any developments which might threaten their illusions. As in most cases of psychofraud, the behaviorists are the victims of their own ideology. They would be merely pitiable if it were not for the fact that they are militant ideologues convinced that they have the means of saving and restructuring the world into whatever shape they wish (137, 138). They seem to have begun a deliberate policy of infiltrating government agencies and universities to further their ends. It is likely that if they could create a Skinnerian utopia, it would be run by practical, evil politicians and not by academic bureaucrats.

Skinnerians quite candidly admit that their form of psychology is akin to religion. No outsider can understand it or appreciate it. The only way to become a full-fledged Skinnerian priest is to have been a student of Skinner or of one of his students and intellectual descendants. It is somewhat like the Catholic Church; only those priests annointed by the Church have the power to annoint new priests.

Skinnerism is a fitting counterfraud to the psychofraud of humanistic psychology. Skinnerism denies subjective behavior. Humanistic psychology gives subjective behavior a central role and almost ignores objectivity. Skinnerism is mechanistic. Humanistic psychology is mystical. Between the two exists the full gamut of psychofraud. An alternative to all psychofraud is Ethical Therapy.

Part Two

ETHICAL THERAPY

5

Foundations

The unexamined life is not worth living for man.
Socrates

Long ago an elderly stonecutter was being tried by the citizens of his community. He was an unusual man in having been a good soldier, teacher, mathematician, art critic, practical physician, scientist and many other professions, although he was not truly outstanding in anything. His principal hobby seemed to be in questioning established "truth" and spreading doubts. He thought this was the road to truth. He was charged with being a corrupter of the morals of the young. It was proved that he questioned the validity of the established religion and the wisdom of the current political and social order. He lived in the freest and most progressive region in the world; yet he clearly sought to undermine its political and social foundations. He had created so much unrest and dissension in the community that he was regarded as a menace to the public welfare by the majority of his peers.

They merely wanted him to stop being a troublemaker and

behave himself. However, the stonecutter felt that in good conscience, he could not refrain from searching for truth as best he could and communicating it to all who were interested. He therefore suggested to the entire community, which had assembled to try him, that the only way they could stop him from being a bother to them was to kill him. They were reluctant to do this because it might have political repercussions and make a martyr out of the stonecutter. But he left them with little choice, and they voted for his execution.

The stonecutter took this with complete calm, which was his usual state of mind, and at no time displayed any adverse emotions. His friends were extremely upset about the turn of events, and they implored him to recant and save his life. However, the stonecutter thought it wrong to compromise his ethics and accommodate to popular prejudice. He said it was better to die in the search of truth than to live in fear. He was executed shortly afterward. He was a recipient and a practitioner of Ethical Therapy. His name was Socrates (16, 107).

About 100 years before Socrates and 6000 miles to the east, there lived another recipient and practitioner of Ethical Therapy who, although unknown to Socrates, would probably have been his best friend had they met. His name was Confucius. He is probably the most influential practitioner of Ethical Therapy who ever lived; although, like all practitioners, he made mistakes.

Confucius was noted for his absolute calm in the face of all adversity and his uncompromising stance on matters of principle, even to the point of his willingness to die for them (30). By his own account, he was never particularly outstanding in any subject, but was well acquainted with all the knowledge of his day (20). He felt that government should be administered only by highly knowledgeable persons with a broad understanding similar to his, because ignorant persons who seek power over others are almost always evil and corrupt. The best safeguard guaranteeing ethical leadership was that the would-be leaders should objectively demonstrate broad knowledge and creativity. He thought that decisions should be based on reason and that emotion had no place in an ethical life. His ideas, although independently derived, were very similar to those of Socrates (20, 30). The difference is that Confucius' ideas were, after a period of 500 years, to serve as the direct basis for one of the most creative civilizations which ever existed. Socrates' ideas survived indirectly through Christianity, which in turn formed the basis for Western Civilization.

Not all recipients and practitioners of Ethical Therapy have been as outstanding or successful as Socrates and Confucius. Some are buried in obscurity and failed to have a noticeable effect on human evolution. Others wavered in making ethical decisions, were plagued by destructive emotions, and on occasion, compromised their principles. Still Ethical Therapy eventually succeeded even in their cases. One such person was Giordano Bruno (1548-1600).

Giordano Bruno was no stranger to psychofraud or destructive emotions. In fact, he became, of his own free will, a Catholic monk in his search for truth. His inquiring mind and passionate nature made it impossible for him to submit to monastic discipline. He became an open heretic, a renegade and a fugitive. He broke all his vows, particularly those related to chastity, and engaged all his passions. His appetite for sensual pleasure as well as his appetite for knowledge seemed to know no bounds. By his own account, "not all the fires of the Caucasus could avail to allay the fires within him." Still his greatest love was the pursuit of truth. As he wandered throughout Europe learning, teaching, fighting, loving, and trying to avoid the Inquisition, he continuously modified and improved his philosophy, which was a coherent view of the universe integrating all the sciences, mathematics, history, and philosophy of his day, as well as theology and other forms of psychofraud which he mistakenly considered knowledge. He came to realize that truth was something one continually sought and not something one found.

When the Inquisition finally caught up with Giordano Bruno, he was a vigorous, mature man of forty-four in the prime of life. He could not bear the thought of dying for theoretical abstractions and an ever-changing philosophy. Therefore, he made an ethical mistake and groveled hysterically before the Inquisition as he recanted his most cherished beliefs. In so doing, he discovered that unethical means cannot achieve ethical ends, and he lived to regret his recantation. He was continuously harassed and made to suffer by the Inquisition for eight years afterward. He finally refused to compromise any further.

At the age of fifty-one, he stated his philosophical position clearly and unequivocally to the Inquisition. He remained absolutely calm and refused to be swayed in the slightest degree by theological arguments or bloody threats. He did this not to defend his ever-changing philosophy, but to defend something much more important: the right of each person to pursue and express truth in his own way to the limits of his capability. As he was being led to the stake, he was offered the solace of a crucifix and of his religion, which he had never really discarded. In a calm, clear voice he rejected this hypocritical offering saying, "Ye who pass judgment on me feel, perhaps, greater fear than myself." He was burned alive and died without uttering a sound. His passionate, tumultuous life ended in the quiet, calm strength that comes from Ethical Therapy.

Thirty-two years after Giordano Bruno was murdered by the Catholic hierarchy, there was born in Holland the man who was most clearly and profoundly to express the nature of, and rationale for, Ethical Therapy. At an early age he began to question all the accepted "truths" of his time and to try to learn as much of mathematics, science, art, and philosophy as he was intellectually capable. He was independently following the same path that had been taken by Confucius, Socrates, Giordano Bruno and countless others. At the age of twenty-four, like his predecessors, he became extremely obnoxious to his community and was forcibly expelled from it. They tried to kill him but failed. He was an extremely versatile young man, however, and had no trouble making his way in the world.

He was a highly skilled optician and artist, besides being an accomplished mathematician, scientist, philosopher, historian, linguist and biblical scholar. He was as quiet, serene and unassuming as Giordano Bruno had been tumultuous, passionate and bombastic. He also had the advantage of having avoided exposure to serious psychofraud from birth and of successfully undergoing Ethical Therapy at a very early age. He was to practice Ethical Therapy all his life. All who knew him commented on his pleasant, courteous and completely unemotional manner in all his dealings. He was noted for his ability to approach any problem in a completely rational, objective and dispassionate manner. He was probably the most unneurotic person who ever lived. He expressed his philosophy, which was pure Ethical Therapy, in a beautiful and great book he called *Etica.* He continuously lived his philosophy and never made any ethical compromises, even when his life depended on this. He risked all his security as well as his life when he refused to recant his "heresies" at the age of twenty-four. He declined a secure, comfortable university appointment at the age of forty-one, because it involved unethical compromises, however minor. He chose instead to continue living in self-imposed poverty and grinding the lenses whose dust he knew was destroying his lungs and would eventually cause his death three years hence.

He chose to die helping men see, rather than to live by unethical compromise. His name was originally Baruch de Spinoza, but he changed it to Benedict when he was excommunicated by the Jewish community of Amsterdam at the age of twenty-four. For hundreds of years after his death, he was to be denounced by the established order as an extremely wicked heretic and a fool. Yet no other person has ever expressed or practiced Ethical Therapy with greater clarity.

Confucius was equally a man of thought and of action. Socrates was a man primarily of thought, but not adverse to action. Giordano Bruno was primarily a man of action, but he could think beautifully. Spinoza was almost entirely a man of thought. Each of these men practiced Ethical Therapy in his own way.

Closer to our own lives we have practitioners and advocates of Ethical Therapy in Thomas Jefferson, Simon Bolivar, Karl Marx, Herbert Spencer, H. G. Wells, Bertrand Russell, Jose Ortega y Gasset, Albert Schweitzer, Dietrich Bonhoeffer, Teilhard de Chardin, Alexander Solzhenitsyn, and thousands of lesser known but equally ethical, if not equally brilliant, persons. These range from the American educator and scientist James B. Conant to the thousands of ordinary persons, who at great personal risk have opposed the stifling of dissent and the free inquiry in the Soviet Union, e.g., Andre Sakharov; to the thousands of Americans who deliberately risked their lives and freedom to oppose the Vietnam war, e.g., Daniel Ellsberg; and to the countless and nameless others who have risked their careers to correct the inequities of bureaucratic corruption in both the communistic and democratic states. The question before us is, What do all these persons have in common?

In examining the lives of all the outstanding practitioners of Ethical Therapy, we find the following three common factors:

1. A broad understanding of *all* the knowledge of their contemporaries. They may not necessarily be outstanding experts in any field of knowledge.
2. The eventual development of a cool, rational and completely unemotional attitude in dealing with *all* problems, even when these persons are by nature highly

emotional. They are unneurotic.

3. A clear understanding and expression of the value that truth is more important than anyone's happiness, including their own and that of their loved ones.

From a purely therapeutic point of view, we would at least like to understand how these persons became unneurotic. Was it an accident of birth? Or was it due to some inadvertent, natural-occurring psychotherapy in their environment? Can persons of ordinary or less than ordinary intelligence also become as unneurotic and creative as these persons? If so, what are the factors which will bring this about? We can easily find common factors in the behavior of healthy, unneurotic persons. But what are the common factors in their heredity and their environment which made them so? We will try to answer all these questions.

Before answering any questions, we must clearly define what the questions really mean and what are our basic goals. We must develop a common language for discussing neuroses and ethics. This is the principal task of this chapter. It may seem somewhat abstract at first, but the relevance of the arguments and the definitions will soon become clear. We begin with a discussion of "method" as it relates to Ethical Therapy.

METHOD

Ethical Therapy is founded not on method but on goals. So long as we are concerned with method, we are vulnerable to psychofraud. Ideologies differ almost entirely in their methods, not in their goals. For example, democracy and communism both claim to want freedom, happiness and prosperity for their citizens. Democracy claims that the basic human freedoms of speech and self-expression are necessary and sufficient conditions for the creation of a progressive society (67, 101). If we do not have these freedoms, we have already lost the game. Communism, according to Lenin, holds that every freedom is a fraud if the means of production are not in the hands of the people (135). Public ownership of the means of production is the most essential ingredient for human progress. Furthermore, the Communist Party as the instrument of the people is infallible in its workings. Therefore, any challenge to the authority or wisdom of the Party is wrong, dangerous and destructive. Any means to suppress these challenges are therefore justified.

The ideology and psychofraud of both democracy and communism consists entirely in accepting as infallible particular means for accomplishing common objectives. The same phenomena occurs in the so-called "social sciences" in general and in psychotherapy in particular. These and other forms of psychofraud become obsessed with method without becoming clear about goals. In order to understand and use Ethical Therapy, we must first understand the nature of goals.

We will develop theory in this chapter and methods of Ethical Therapy in the following chapters. It is conceivable that both the theory and the methods may be in error. Only the basic goals are beyond error, because basic goals are beyond logic. To accept blindly the methods and theory of Ethical Therapy as true is merely another type of psychofraud, because these methods and theory have yet to be fully tested scientifically. It is only by accepting the *goals* of Ethical Therapy that we can achieve lasting mental health and avoid all psychofraud and neuroses.

GOALS

We all have goals and purposes. Most persons seem to have the negative goal of avoiding pain and death. Yet we know that sadomasochists seek pain and suicides seek death.*

* In discussing suicide we refer only to those persons who have a serious interest in killing themselves, not persons who go through sham suicides as a means of getting sympathy and attention.

It seems impossible to get people to agree on goals. Therefore, we might be unrealistic to expect them to agree on methods. However, the apparent disagreement on goals is only superficial. This disagreement results from the fact that most stated goals are, in truth, merely means of achieving what are the basic common goals of all humanity.

We say that a goal is "basic" when it is an end in itself and not a means to an end. A goal is basic when it is all that we want and we wish nothing beyond it. In this context a suicide's basic goal might not be death *per se* but the elimination of all sensation and desire. The suicide might want to eliminate sensations because they are unbearably painful, e.g., a terminal cancer patient or a victim of torture. Desire *in general* might be eliminated because some *particular* desire cannot be fulfilled, e.g., suicide because of unrequited love. A shorthand way of expressing all of this is to say that a person commits suicide to eliminate unhappiness.

We define *happiness* as "a state of mind in which we *feel* that our desires *are being* fulfilled." Desires that *have been* fulfilled do not make us happy. Only desires that *are being* fulfilled make us happy. Desires that are not being fulfilled make us unhappy. Since it is usually impossible for any person to simultaneously fulfill all his desires, most persons are usually happy and unhappy at the same time. When the strength and number of the desires being fulfilled exceeds the strength and number of desires unfulfilled, we say "the person is happy." When the converse is the case, we say "the person is unhappy."

It seems that happiness is a basic goal for all human beings. Other desires are intermediate goals whose fulfillment is merely a means toward this basic goal. Our desires themselves are determined by our heredity and then modified by our environment. The desire to remove the basic sensation of hunger is innate. However, the desire for a particular kind of food is learned, although many tastes are innately pleasing while other tastes are innately obnoxious. We are not born wanting food. We are born wanting to end pain caused by the absence of food. In Maslow's sense, pleasure and the avoidance of pain are basic needs. In Skinner's sense, stimuli which cause our subjective sense of pleasure or pain are respectively rewards and punishments. They are reinforcers, not because of our subjective feelings, but because they can modify our behavior. However, we each know what pain and pleasure are, even if Skinnerians might deny their existence.

As human beings develop, the stimuli which cause pain and pleasure change. For example, a hungry child might feel pain from the lack of food and pleasure from its ingestion. However, certain ascetics feel neither pain nor pleasure in regard to food. They may eat only as a logically perceived means of staying alive. The need for food, i.e., the reinforcing properties of food, can also be eliminated by drugs and brain surgery without any learning on the part of the person (140). Such a person might still wish to be happy, but he would no longer have a desire for food. In the case of the ascetic, food and perhaps life itself are merely means to an end and not ends in themselves; i.e., they are not basic goals.

Happiness, in our context, can be caused by, but is not synonymous with, the absence of pain and the presence of pleasure. Fulfilling a desire may cause pain and give no pleasure but still bring about happiness—for example, a mother giving birth to a desired child. Pain and pleasure are physiologically determined mental states which can be experimentally induced by directly stimulating certain parts of the brain (140). They are, therefore, not usually basic goals but merely means of producing the apparent basic goal of happiness. The question before us is whether happiness is the only basic goal.

Basic Goals

Happiness is clearly a basic goal. Some would say that it is the only basic goal. However, happiness is an unoperational goal, because one person's happiness can be another person's unhappiness, e.g., sadomasochism. If happiness is a purely personal experience determined by our peculiar heredity and experiences, then happiness cannot serve as a practical guide for implementing a scientific ethical system or psychotherapy. We cannot agree with the ethical hedonists that "the greatest good is what makes for the greatest happiness for the greatest number," because we cannot agree on which kind of happiness is best. Not even the humanistic psychologists who claim that all happiness is good would approve encouraging sadists to do their thing, unless perhaps they chose to do it to masochists. However, as is well known, when the masochist said, "Hurt me!" the sadist said, "No!" Therefore, happiness would be a nonoperational basic goal, even if it were the only basic goal.

Animals can probably never go beyond pleasure and pain as means of inducing or preventing happiness. Human beings, however, can and often do go beyond the pleasure principle. They do this by creating their own basic goals (150).

While we may all be born with happiness as a basic goal, we clearly do not always keep it as a basic goal. For example, there are religious persons who believe in an absolute morality, which they will uphold irrespective of who is made happy or unhappy by it. They will undergo extreme privation and even die or kill their loved ones to uphold their religious principles, e.g., the biblical myth of Abraham's willingness to sacrifice his son.

It might be argued that following ethical principles is really increasing happiness. This may or may not be the case in the beginning of any form of ethical behavior. What is important is that ethical behavior can become an end in itself, i.e., a basic goal. An ethical person, regardless of his particular ethics, behaves as he does without any thought for his or anyone else's happiness. Whatever the cause-and-effect relationships between ethics and happiness, they are clearly distinct entities. Happiness is a specific state of mind. Ethics are a particular set of behavioral rules.

ETHICS

Ethics exist on both an objective and subjective level. Subjectively, ethics are rules which we feel compelled to follow irrespective of their emotional effects. We will follow these rules whether they cause us or anyone else pain or pleasure. We will follow these rules whether they will cause us or anyone else anger or sorrow. No subhuman animal can behave this way. This is what is called the "Moral Sense." It is what makes us uniquely human. It can and has been the source of misery and joy for millions of persons.

The Moral Sense can create saints and martyrs, but it also can create oppressors and tyrants. The Moral Sense can produce men such as Confucius, Buddha, Socrates, Jesus, Spinoza, Gandhi, and Schweitzer; but it can also produce a Torquemada, a Calvin, a Robespierre, a Lenin, and a Hitler. When a person becomes utterly convinced that he is righteous, he may die for his beliefs, but he often is also willing to kill those who do not share his beliefs. Therefore, *subjective ethics* alone are inadequate for guiding human behavior. We need *objective ethics.*

Ludwig Wittgenstein, one of the greatest twentieth-century philosophers, claimed that ethical principles could not be derived objectively (167, 168, 169). He argued, quite convincingly, that if a person were to know all the facts in the world, they would not tell him how he *ought* to behave in general, although they might tell him how he *should* behave as a means of achieving some particular goal. In other words, facts can tell us how to achieve goals, but they cannot tell us what our basic goals should be. If human beings had an infinity of distinct basic goals, we would have to agree with Wittgenstein and say that ethics can never be objectively determined. However, as we will show, there are only two basic goals, and all other goals and desires are merely means of achieving these two basic goals.

We know that happiness is a basic goal because we never speak of our own happiness as a means to any other end. The very question, Why do you want to be happy, makes no sense. Happiness is an end in itself. We can ask a person, Why do you desire food, sex, money, power, knowledge, or death, and these questions will make sense, since they can be seen to be direct or indirect means to happiness. They are means of avoiding pain and receiving pleasure. However, happiness is never a means to any other end. Therefore, happiness is a basic goal common to all persons.

Taking as true the proposition that happiness is a basic goal, it then follows that any goal which can be substituted for happiness is also a basic goal. This is the case because if happiness is an end in itself, then anything we desire in its place will also have to be an end in itself.

We know that pleasure is always a source of happiness and that pain is always a source of unhappiness. Therefore, anyone who is willing to forego pleasure and undergo pain with no hope of ever receiving pleasure again has as a basic goal something other than happiness. This applies to aberrant persons, such as sadomasochists, who receive pleasure from activities which usually cause pain in others. This does *not* apply to persons who forego pleasure for the moment and undergo temporary pain in the hope of greater future pleasure while avoiding greater pain. For example, the Christian martyr who undergoes privation, torture and death for his beliefs in the hope of avoiding Hell and then going to Heaven is still pursuing the basic goal of happiness. It is the martyr who does not believe in a better life after death and still avoids pleasure, suffers pain and dies for his principles who has found a basic goal other than happiness.

Historically we have examples of such persons in Confucius, Socrates, Bruno, Spinoza, Jefferson and Trotsky (30,

32, 99, 101, 143). None of these men expected a better afterlife. Indeed, they all disclaimed the existence of such a thing. Yet we know that they all took great risks and underwent privations; some even underwent imprisonment and suffered pain and death, all for rather abstract ethical principles.

As we examine the life histories of other persons known to have behaved in a similar manner, we see that always what they substituted for the basic goal of happiness was ethical principle. Yet we know that many of their beliefs were very different. As we look deeper, however, we find one common belief in all of them. They all shared the belief that truth is more important than happiness and that the preservation and expansion of truth is worth any risk or any price.

The only basic goal that has ever been substituted for happiness is the goal of truth for ourselves and for others. This is the case even when the notions of "what is true" and "how can we know truth" are very different.

We note that the substitution of truth for happiness as a basic goal does not preclude truth's causing happiness or unhappiness. If a person has truth as his basic goal, then by definition the expansion of truth will make him happy. The important distinction is that he pursues truth as an end in itself and not as a means to an end. He would have pursued truth even if it had made him unhappy. He does not concern himself with the emotional effects of truth in his pursuit of it.

The ethics of truth is the only basic goal which can be substituted for happiness. The only objective ethics are those ethics based on the maximization of truth. "That which maximizes truth is the greatest good" is an objective ethical principle which can be used to guide human behavior and at the same time maximize happiness. Objective ethics are therefore uniformly optimal rules of behavior. They are those principles which, regardless of our basic goals, truth or happiness, will maximize both truth and happiness. They are principles which will best fulfill our basic desires, irrespective of whatever our immediate desires may be. To see that this is the case, we must first explore the nature of truth.

Truth

To possess truth is to know. But how do we know when we know? Clearly subjective "truth," i.e., the belief that we know, is inadequate, since people can believe many contradictory things which are at variance with reality. This is abundantly manifested in religious wars and in psychotic behavior. Therefore, an objective ethics cannot be founded on subjective truth.

Subjective truth is the basis of all mystical experience. A "mystical experience" is a type of personal enlightenment which convinces us that we know in the absence of any objective evidence. This is how, according to legend, Buddha discovered truth while sitting under a tree engaged in contemplation. It is what the Gestalt psychologists would call "insight." This type of mystical enlightenment is the basis of many great discoveries. Creative scientists and inventors as well as artists often have these periods of insight during which a pattern crystallizes. Therefore, subjective truth is probably a necessary first step in the discovery of objective truth. The problem arises when persons *substitute* subjective truth for objective truth.

We often hear of the mystical nature of our great thinkers —Pascal, Newton, Goethe, William James, and Einstein, among others. However, it is often forgotten that persons such as Torquemada, Calvin, Rasputin and Hitler were also mystics. Therefore, while subjective truth can lead to objective truth, it can also lead to gross self-deception and a destruction of objective truth. It can lead to psychofraud. The only way to assure the maximum expansion of truth is to subject *all* assertions of truth to objective tests before *tentatively* accepting our own insights, let alone the insights of others. This does not mean that we reject subjectivity and personal enlightenment as means toward objective truth. It means that we remain skeptical about *all* "revelations" and accept models, theories, and hypotheses as true only insofar as they can be objectively verified.

Objective Truth

Objectively, the only time we know that we know is when our alleged knowledge enables us to predict and control. We objectively accepted Newton's mystical insights into the workings of the universe because those insights enabled us to predict and eventually control astronomical phenomena with great precision and reliability.* We accepted Einstein's mystical insights into nature because these insights enabled us to predict and control even better than Newton's insights. Similarly, many of us reject the insights of the Indian mystics because there is no objective evidence that these insights enabled anyone to predict and control as well as the systematic application of scientific method. We reject pure mysticism and all forms of psychofraud because they simply do not work in the objective world.

Scientific method is a technique for assuring that mystical insights and theories in general are objectively valid. If reading Tarot cards, Ouija boards, tea leaves, astrological charts, or inkblots increases our ability to predict and control, then scientific method will lead to the acceptance of the proposition that these mystical techniques have some validity. Scientific method demands controlled experimentation to verify all models. Subjective belief and clinical evidence are inadequate criteria for truth (50).

Scientific method can never give us certainty, because all measurements, observations and experiments are liable to have errors. Therefore, scientific method can only give us

* The creation of artificial satellites and space flight in general represent a control of astronomical phenomena.

probable knowledge. Only mystics presume certainty. Alleged "scientists" who claim certainty are themselves being mystical. Systematic doubt is the basis of science and objective truth.

Since objective truth is probabilistic and not certain, objective ethics cannot be absolute, but must be relative. Truth itself is an unknowable ideal to which we can always get closer but which we can never fully reach.* It is an asymptotic process. That is objectively true which enables us to predict and control. That is "truest" which *best* enables us to predict and control. From past experience and the nature of the universe, we know that what is truest today may not be truest tomorrow.

The basic goal of pursuing objective truth is an infinite process which has no end. This is the case because (1) that which must be known, i.e., predicted and controlled, is itself infinite in time and space, i.e., the universe; and (2) we can never reduce our observational errors to zero about any aspect of nature. It is the unreachable, infinite nature of ultimate objective truth that makes its pursuit a uniformly optimal strategy.

* When we speak of "truth," we refer to truth about nature (the physical, biological and the psychosocial environment). In the artificial world of mathematics, we may know absolute truth through tautological statements, but even here we can make semantic errors. A few years ago a famous mathematician "proved" a very complex theorem which was widely held to be absolutely true by the mathematical community until another mathematician gave a counter example of the theorem. This was a *scientific* proof that an alleged *analytic* proof was in error. Therefore, we should even doubt apparently tautological statements such as "Business is business," in which the same word might be used in different senses, thereby producing semantic errors.

Optimality

Given that (1) our basic goal is to expand objective truth and (2) only that which enables us to predict and control is objectively true, then only that which increases our ability to predict and control is "good." Since (1) what we predict and control is our total environment and (2) the total environment is infinite in temporal and spatial extension, we can determine how "good" an action was only by integrating its effects over all future time and space. Since science indicates that our lives are finite and our knowledge dies with us,* truth can continue to exist if and only if we communicate it to others. Mysticism can justify the sole pursuit of personal, subjective truth. Objective ethics justifies only the pursuit of objective truth which can be, and should be, communicated to others. Therefore, if our basic goal is objective truth, then we are concerned with truth for everyone and not just for ourselves. We may emphasize truth for ourselves, but ethically we can neither ignore truth for others nor increase our own knowledge at the expense of other persons' knowledge and welfare. If we are to be ethical, we must try to maximize truth in the collective body of mankind which extends into the future. Clearly truth is never collectively maximized by any action which reduces truth for a single person. To increase truth is to increase the collective ability of all persons to predict and control their total environment. To reduce truth is to reduce the ability of any person to crea-

* We note that all the scientific studies attempting to show the persistence of the ego after death have been negative. These studies range from the investigations of William James to those of Houdini and Dr. Rhine at Duke University. Even the Soviets are currently investigating these phenomena with similar results. See *Psychic Discoveries Behind the Iron Curtain* by S. Ostrander and L. Schroeder, Prentice-Hall, 1970.

tively predict and control the total environment.

A mere book or a computer may contain valid information, but truth cannot exist independently of persons. If we value truth, then we must value the persons who are the repositories, disseminators and creators of truth. Truth is information which has become part of the collective intelligence of humanity (50). To diminish truth for any person, including ourself, is to diminish it for all humanity. To increase truth for any person, including ourself, is to increase it for all humanity. However, only the truth we engender in others survives our lives. Therefore, truth cannot be maximized if it is not communicated to others and continuously made to grow through creativity.

By maximizing truth we will maximize happiness, because truth is the only inexhaustible desire whose pursuit can always make us happy. All other desires become satiated and disappear. If our basic desire is happiness, we must then find new desires to satisfy. In an affluent, hedonistic society, the desire for desire becomes the overwhelming need, which drives persons to drugs, mysticism and psychofraud in general. This desire for desire is a frustrating, futile goal which leads to disillusionment and unhappiness for those who seek it. The pursuit of happiness as an end in itself leads only to unhappiness. Happiness can only come about indirectly by leading a meaningful, purposeful life. Only the pursuit of objective truth for ourselves and others as an end in itself can give continued meaning and purpose to life.

Regardless of what our immediate and basic desires may be, we will best achieve them by pursuing truth as an end in itself. By dedicating our lives to the pursuit of objective truth we maximize both truth and happiness. Therefore, the adoption of objective truth as our sole basic goal is a uniformly optimal strategy which will get us whatever we want better than any other strategy.

To be ethical is to desire objective truth at least as much as happiness. The more overriding our desire for truth is, the more ethical we become. When objective truth is a person's sole basic goal, then he has reached his maximum level of ethics and we say the person is "moral." When a person desires happiness more than truth, then he is unethical. When his *sole* basic desire is happiness, he is at his lowest level of ethics, and we say the person is "immoral."

MORALITY

A person who is ethical may occasionally behave unethically, just as a person who is unethical may occasionally behave ethically. Ethical persons increase truth more than they decrease it, and so the net effect of their lives is the increase of truth. Unethical persons decrease truth more than they increase it, and so the net effect of their lives is the decrease of truth. Moral persons only increase truth and never decrease it. Immoral persons only decrease truth and never increase it.

It should be noted that a person has three and only three options in regard to truth: he can (1) increase truth, (2) decrease truth, and (3) not affect truth. In real life almost everything we do will either increase or decrease truth. Trivia is, therefore, an ideal concept which is used in a relative sense for actions which have *very little* effect on truth. Similarly, in real life almost no one becomes totally moral or immoral. These are also ideal concepts which are used in a relative sense to describe persons who are highly ethical and highly unethical respectively. Absolute morality is a state to which we can always get closer as we become increasingly ethical, but we can never fully reach it without a quantum jump across the threshold of morality. Ethical Therapy can help us make this quantum jump.

Ethical Therapy is a process for increasing morality. Morality is the desire for truth. Morality is the basis of all creativity. The more ethical a person is the more creative he will be for a given level of intelligence. By seeking objective truth as our *sole* goal, we maximize creativity, because truth can only grow when there is creativity.

CREATIVITY

We defined *creativity* as "the organization of the environment into new patterns which increase the collective ability of mankind to predict and control the total environment." By this definition any new technology or scientific discovery is a product of creative endeavor. However, teaching truth is also creative because here we have organized the environment, i.e., the student's mind, into a new pattern which increases his ability to predict and control his total environment.

By similar reasoning, works of art are also a result of creativity because their perception reorganizes persons' minds into new patterns which increase their ability to predict and control. In the case of the effects of art, the reorganization occurs mainly at the unconscious level as opposed to the conscious reorganizations of science, technology and teaching. However, the result is the same. The greater the art perceived, the greater the increase in the ability to predict and control the total environment. The reasoning behind the creative nature of the artistic processes is discussed elsewhere (50). However, the fact that exposure to great art increases the ability to predict and control could be objectively demonstrated by controlled experiments.

Hypothesis: Children raised in an environment replete with great art, e.g., the music of Bach, Beethoven and Penderecki, the paintings of El Greco, Rembrandt and Picasso, and the literature of Shakespeare, Dostoyevsky and Solzhenitsyn, should be better able to predict and control their total environment than a statistically matched group of children raised in a similar environment devoid of artistic stimuli. Although a controlled experiment of this nature has never been done, there is considerable clinical evidence that this is the case (50).

The above hypothesized relationships between truth and artistic beauty need scientific verification. For the time being we will use these stated relationships merely as working hypotheses. Intuitively we subscribe to the ancient wisdom that truth is beauty, and beauty is truth.

As was indicated earlier, creativity is the best evidence of health. It is also the best objective evidence of ethics. Unethical persons, i.e., persons who have happiness as their prime basic goal, are by definition uncreative in their net effects and may be destructive. To destroy is to *disorganize* the environment into patterns which *decrease* our ability to predict and control the total environment.

Since unethical persons are at best uncreative and at worst destructive, it is unethical to waste energy by increasing their ability to predict and control. The net effect of increasing the ability of unethical persons to predict and control is to decrease the collective ability of humanity to predict and control. Immoral persons are by definition always destructive and should always be avoided. By avoiding unethical persons, we increase the collective creativity of the human race. This is the case because by avoiding unethical and immoral persons we deprive them of intelligence and the power to destroy, since they can only obtain power and intelligence by using the creativity of other persons for their own purposes. Since the net effect of unethical persons is destructive, denying them intelligence and power decreases destruction, i.e., increases creativity. These relationships are expressed in the following equation:

Equation 1: $C \simeq IE$

Where: C = Creativity, in quanta of knowledge generated per hour, Range: $(-\infty, \infty)$

I = Intelligence, in quanta of knowledge controlled per hour, Range: $(0, \infty)$
E = Ethics, dimensionless ratio Range: (-1, 0) for an unethical person, (0, 1) for an ethical person, -1 for an immoral person, 0 for a trivial person, 1 for a moral person.
$\simeq$ Indicates an approximation
Destructiveness is negative creativity

As is indicated in Equation 1, creativity is a function of both ethics and intelligence. Recall that intelligence is the ability to predict and control the total environment. All ethical persons are creative. However, a highly ethical person of low intelligence may not be as creative as a less ethical person of high intelligence. Since a moral person has truth as his *sole* basic goal, he considers neither his nor anyone else's happiness when making decisions or taking actions. He is always creative.

Moral persons are probably quite rare in human history. When they appear, they seem to shake the world with their creativity. Most of the founders of the great world religions and ethical systems seem to have been highly ethical men whose work became corrupted by the less ethical men who succeeded them. This seems to have been the case with Moses, Confucius, Zarathustra, Buddha, Jesus, Mohammed, and Luther. In our own day, we have seen it happen to Marx.

Moral persons may be highly creative even when their intelligence is less than extraordinary. However, it seems to take a minimum intelligence of a fairly high order to become moral, just as it takes a human level of intelligence to become ethical. Clearly no subhuman animal is ethical, because no subhuman animal creates systematically. When unethical persons are highly intelligent, they use their ability to predict and control to destroy. Immoral persons are usually highly intelligent and highly destructive.

From our definitions it follows that highly ethical persons are healthy and that unethical persons are neurotic. Examples of highly intelligent, unethical men in our own time are Stalin and Hitler. Both were neurotic. Hitler, who was probably more intelligent and imaginative than Stalin, was also more neurotic, unethical and destructive. The relationships between ethics, intelligence, creativity, neurosis and Ethical Therapy may now be discussed.

6

Applications

The previous chapter developed a general ethical theory at a somewhat abstract, but still simple, nonrigorous level. In this and subsequent chapters we will discuss how these abstractions can be applied to our everyday lives in order to become less neurotic and more creative. In order to obviate the necessity of continuously referring to the previous and subsequent chapters, the basic definitions, axioms and theorems of psychofraud and Ethical Therapy are summarized in the Appendix. These include points which are still to be developed in this and the following chapters.

THERAPY AND ETHICS

Systems of ethics and psychotherapy have in common the fact that they both try to change human behavior. Some psychotherapies claim that they are "value free"; however, this is often a specious claim since virtually all psychothera-

pists differentiate between normal and abnormal behavior.*
This is a value judgement.

Ethical Therapy does not try to change basic values but rather redirects the person to emphasize the innate value of objective truth and deemphasize the innate value of happiness. When the person has no value other than objective truth, Ethical Therapy has fully succeeded and can go no farther.

In practicing Ethical Therapy it must always be kept in mind that this, like psychotherapy, is a special type of education. The object of Ethical Therapy is to replace information which decreases objective truth, i.e., decreases our ability to predict and control, with information which increases objective truth. This may not be possible when the person already values happiness above truth. When this is the case, the person will resist the elimination of delusions which make him happy. Some distortions of reality may be altered, if this does not adversely affect his happiness. However, neither Ethical Therapy nor any other treatment is likely to alter the basic value that happiness is more important than truth. For this reason unethical persons can probably never be made ethical and mentally healthy. They have irreversible entropy.

Entropy

Intuitively "entropy" is the decrease in the order and coherent information of a system. When we take a sculpture and smash it to pieces we have increased the entropy of that system. When a book is burned, the entropy in that system has increased. When a living creature is ill or damaged, then that system has increased its entropy. When a living creature

* Some of the fringe humanistic psychologists consider all behavior "normal," apparently even that of homocidal psychopaths.

dies, then it has reached maximum irreversible entropy. The second law of thermodynamics states that in all closed systems the entropy is always increasing, i.e., entropy is always irreversible. However, this law, like all scientific laws, is only an approximation to reality.

Every system is in various ways connected to every other system. The universe is an interconnected whole. Therefore, no system is ever completely closed, including the universe (51). However, some systems, such as the solar system, appear to be, for all practical purposes, closed, since they are very little affected by outside forces. Living creatures are also, in a sense, closed and autonomous; however, they appear to violate the second law of thermodynamics.

Living creatures clearly decrease their entropy as they grow, i.e., they increase their coherent information. Eventually all life forms begin to decay and die; therefore, the second law eventually catches up with all of us. However, while they are growing, the information content of all life forms is increasing. This is shown in part by an increase in the size of the body, but most notably by an increase in the information content of the nervous system, which becomes increasingly complex as animals mature. Even if the actual number of nerve cells decreases, each individual cell and the connections between them become increasingly complex as the organism grows. A concomittant of this is an increase in the ability of the animal to predict and control.

An obvious explanation of this phenomenon is that living creatures are in dynamic contact with the rest of the environment and that they increase their information content by taking information from the rest of the environment and making it become a part of themselves. Nutrition is an obvious example of this. Learning is a less obvious example. In laboratory experiments it can be shown that the net entropy of a closed or nearly closed system which contains and includes living growing creatures is in fact increasing. However, human evolution has another component. Man is creative; he can produce more information than he consumes, although he may not always do so. That this is the case involves very complex arguments beyond the scope of this book but which are presented elsewhere (51). The fact is that man can overcome entropy through ethics.

Evolution in the larger sense involves a decrease in the entropy of the biomass, not necessarily in the solar system. While the increase in the coherent information of the biomass may be at the expense of the useful energy of the rest of the solar system, the evolution of man can transcend dependence on the solar system, as has been shown (50, 51). This transcendence results from ethics.

Objective ethics are systems of optimal behavioral rules for decreasing the entropy of a sentient species.* Another way of saying the same thing is that ethics are rules for best increasing the total coherent information content, i.e., objective truth in the human species. This is most clearly shown in the cultural evolution of our species. When segments of the human species, such as civilizations, systematically incorporate unethical rules of behavior, either de facto or de jure, then such segments have irreversible entropy and they die, usually at the hands of a more progressive civilization. In this way ethical and psychosocial evolution progress through natural selection. The essential difference between unethical and ethical civilizations is that the former puts a higher premium on happiness than on objective truth, while the latter puts a higher premium on objective truth. We have examples of ancient ethical civilizations, such as the Sumerians, the Egyptians, the Greeks, and the Indians, which were, as societies, highly creative and which then became entropic. All of these societies became highly mystical and became

* A "sentient" organism is an organism which is creative; it can predict and control its own ability to predict and control.

obsessed with subjective truth and happiness as they began to undergo ethical decay.

Although all civilizations have had mystical *components* at all times, it may be *generalized* that *all* civilizations become *highly* mystical just before they begin to undergo irreversible entropy. They have institutionalized their psychofraud in an irreversible process which turns the society into a closed system and eventually results in the destruction of that civilization by unavoidable outside reality. This is beginning to happen to Western Civilization today.

How and why this happens is discussed elsewhere (50, 51). The important points to be made here are that (1) from an evolutionary, ethical point of view, it is best that entropic systems destroy themselves and (2) individual human beings represent a microcosm of the evolution and entropic decay of human societies. Human societies decay only because individual persons decay until unethical persons represent a growing majority of the population. At this point the civilization in effect commits suicide (50). Similarly, when an individual person has incorporated a majority of psychofraudulent models into his mind, he in effect commits ethical suicide by closing his mind to outside reality.

The entropic decay of the person begins when he makes a *choice* to seek happiness at the expense of objective truth. For young children this is not a choice which can be made, because the alternatives are not yet clear. Therefore, young children are all ethical and grow in creativity. But sometime after early adolescence most persons seem to make an ethical choice. Once the choice is made, either consciously or unconsciously, then the entropic person will tend to avoid any situation which will increase objective truth at the expense of his happiness. Since it is not possible to maintain illusions of happiness without maintaining illusions about one's self and one's relationship to the universe, the unethical person will incorporate ideology and psychofraud as ways of maintaining his illusions. He will resist violently any threat to his illusions by persecuting ideological heretics or at least avoiding them. It should be noted that although all unethical persons are filled with illusions and need neurotic illusions to be happy, not all persons who have illusions and are neurotic are unethical. Ethical persons abandon their illusions when they see that they are in conflict with objective truth. They become less neurotic. Unethical persons create new illusions when confronted with unpleasant objective truth. They become ever more neurotic and destructive.

The above is clearly seen in religious persecutions when unethical religious authorities have temporal power. We see it today in the Soviet Union where one form of psychofraud—the Orthodox church, Czarism, etc.—was replaced through force by another—communism. It is interesting to speculate what type of society might have been created by a group of psychotherapists with a common form of psychofraud, if they were given temporal power. Skinner has already indicated the type of society he would create. So far his political naiveté has spared us one more enforced form of psychofraud. However, for the unethical person, this is not the problem. He is his own worst enemy.

Since the unethical person, by definition, seeks happiness above objective truth, he can only accept objective truth when it does not cause him unhappiness. Since neuroses, by definition, stem from the incorporation of false information which makes us happy at the cost of decreasing our ability to predict and control the *total* environment, it logically follows that the unethical person cannot decrease his neurosis. He has become a semiclosed system with irreversible entropy. His attempts to be happy at any cost may eventually make him miserable, but he cannot demolish his illusions once he is on this track. He can only incorporate information which does not cause him unhappiness. He cannot replace the information which produced his neuroses with objective truth.

We can never be certain as to who is ethical or unethical. Therefore, all persons should be treated as if they are ethical until we have overwhelming evidence to the contrary. But it follows logically that if a person is indeed unethical he cannot benefit from Ethical Therapy in any way, since it will at best only make him unhappy. He may benefit unethically from conventional psychotherapy by being made happy with some new illusions or the reinforcement of his old ones. However, this will not increase his creativity or reduce his neuroses. Unethical persons have ceased to be part of the open evolving system which is humanity; they are beyond the help of Ethical Therapy. They have permanently programmed themselves to be neurotic. However, we all seem to be preprogrammed by our genes to be ethical.

Programming

Programming refers to the systematic encoding of information into a system. The human mind is programmed in two ways, (1) by the basic genetic code and (2) by the environment. Our basic genetic program directs us to seek happiness and truth. The Moral Sense causes unhappiness when we are not expanding truth. Through random or planned environmental techniques of reward and punishment, we can become reprogrammed to satisfy the demands of our innate moral program through psychofraud and other forms of self-delusion and thereby indulge almost exclusively in our desires for happiness. When this happens, we become unethical and neurotic. Through similar techniques we can learn that the greatest happiness comes from the expansion of objective truth until we clearly value truth above happiness. When this happens, we become ethical, healthy and creative.

While the mind is almost certainly an effect of the body, particularly the brain, it is also clear that the mind can affect the body. This is demonstrated in psychosomatic illness, hypnosis and conditioning. Therefore, the mind can reprogram itself. It can reprogram itself to become increasingly unethical or ethical. But, for reasons given in the previous sections, the unethical person has lost his ability for autoprogramming in the ethical direction. He has irreversible entropy.

Our ability for autoprogramming is itself dependent on the outside forces of heredity and environment. Therefore, our freedom of will is relative and not absolute. However, this uniquely human capability for self-programming, which is a consequence of the genetically programmed Moral Sense, enables us to grow in ethical intelligence and creative power so long as we have not perverted the Moral Sense by becoming unethical. Through reprogramming we can overcome our most primitive instincts and emotions, which are neurologically tied to the pleasure centers of the brain and are part of our program to be happy.*

EMOTIONS

Emotions are preprogrammed patterns of behavior which predispose us to react to situations (1) aggressively, (2) fearfully, or (3) lovingly. To react aggressively to a situation is to seek to destroy, injure, or remove the source of the situation. For example, if someone shoots at us, an aggressive response is to kill, wound or otherwise incapacitate that person, for example, by shackling or imprisonment.

To react fearfully to a situation is to remove ourselves from the situation or to surrender to it. For example, if someone shoots at us, a fearful reaction would be to run,

* Our basic emotions and pleasure centers are directly controlled by the primitive, prehuman part of the brain and are apparently affected by the purely human, i.e., neocritical, parts of the brain only in an inhibitory capacity (125, 139, 140).

hide, or surrender and put ourselves at the mercy of the person shooting.

To react lovingly to a situation is to reinforce the source of the situation and help it along. For example, if someone shoots at us, a loving response would be to present ourselves as a more visible target or better still, walk up to the person doing the shooting, put the gun against us and pull the trigger.

It is in the nature of emotions that *normally* (1) aggressive acts generate only aggression or fear, (2) fearful acts generate opportunistic aggression through the display of weakness, fear through contagion or love through sympathy, (3) loving acts generate only love through mutual reinforcement. Neutral situations generate indifference. All situations are seen as aggressive, fearful, loving, or neutral. Therefore, one would ordinarily say that, the Gospels notwithstanding, a person who reacts lovingly when someone shoots at him deliberately is highly neurotic or abnormal, while the aggressive and fearful responses may be normal and healthy. Similarly, to react aggressively or fearfully to a loving situation is also neurotic. Other emotions, such as sorrow, envy, greed, sympathy, and anger, are variations on and combinations of the three prime emotions previously identified.

While the common concept of "emotion" usually includes all these notions, it also includes other vague notions such as "strong subjective feelings," "agitated passions," "extreme joy or happiness" and such specific physiological states as hunger, sexual arousal and pain. However, the definition of emotion given here is quite specific and does *not* include these other vague notions. A person may be in any or all of these aforementioned states without necessarily experiencing emotion. Furthermore, two persons can behave in exactly the same way in a given situation; yet one person could be motivated by logic while the other person was motivated by emotion. We cannot necessarily infer emotional states from objective behavior. Emotions may someday be able to be put in a one-to-one correspondence with specific physiological states. But until then and perhaps even afterward, we should consider emotion a purely subjective state.

The best objective indicator of destructive emotions is evidenced when a person systematically behaves in such a way that he defeats his own purpose, e.g., when a person kills a "loved" one out of jealousy or commits suicide out of self-pity. This type of behavior is usually called irrational and not merely illogical. Emotionally determined behavior can also be perfectly rational, ethical and creative, as in the case of maternal love or aggressive self-defense against destructive persons. However, we cannot be creative in our emotions sometimes without also being destructive at other times. For example, we may creatively love someone, but at the same time we may be destructively possessive of that person, if we are being guided by our emotions. Emotions can give us benefits—but at a price. Only objective ethics can guide us through life without these contradictions. Only objective ethics can help us overcome destructive emotions, by making all decisions on the basis of what is logically and scientifically ethical and not on the basis of emotional compulsion.

Behavior can be evaluated by objective ethics. Emotions can only be inferred when a person systematically behaves irrationally and contrary to his stated purposes. As long as a person behaves ethically, we cannot be sure whether or not he is emotional. Although we cannot objectively demonstrate emotions, we each know that emotions exist in ourselves because we perceive our own thoughts directly. We logically infer emotions in others from their objective behavior because we can see the relationship between our own emotions and our own behavior. We are most prone to error when we assume specific causes for emotions, as in the case of psychoanalysis.

Given that emotions are real* and represent a double-edged sword that can induce both creative and destructive behavior, we are left with the following questions: (1) How can we eliminate destructive emotions? (2) If we eliminate destructive emotions, what happens to creative emotions? and (3) Is there an adequate substitute for creative emotions? We will try to answer all these questions in the following sections and chapters.

The important thing to keep in mind about emotions is that they are preprogrammed. When we react emotionally, we do not reason and logically decide on our course of action. We do what we do automatically, because of certain preprogramming in our nervous system. The only logic involved is in determining whether the situation is aggressive, fearful or loving, and in how we will accomplish our purposes. In our example, the situation was aggressive. However, an insult is also a form of aggression which is more psychological than physical. A fearful situation would be created if we encountered someone screaming in terror and running for his life, but a mere verbal threat may also produce fear. A loving situation would be created if we encountered someone offering us shelter, sustenance, and companionship; however, mere words of kindness may produce a loving situation. We learn from experience which situations are aggressive, fearful or loving. Even the interpretation of a situation may be preprogrammed; it may not involve conscious logic.

Such is the case with chickens who react fearfully to a hawk silhouette even when they have never seen a hawk before, or the fearful reaction of almost all healthy mammals to sudden loud noises even when they have never heard a loud noise before. In this case, both the interpretation and

* We note that a true Skinnerian behaviorist would deny, or at least ignore, the existence of emotions.

the reaction are preprogrammed. They have been synthesized by the genes and not by experience.

From an evolutionary point of view, it is clear that preprogrammed emotion and interpretation had considerable advantages in natural selection. Chickens who responded automatically to a hawk silhouette were more likely to survive and reproduce than chickens who had to learn from experience that hawks were dangerous. Primitive men who responded aggressively or fearfully to aggressive situations were more likely to survive and reproduce than men who had to learn about these things by trial and error. Mothers who responded lovingly to the fears of their children were more likely to help them survive so that they could become reproductive adults. Humans who were loving toward one another were more likely to help each other survive, mate, and raise healthy children. Therefore, genetically programmed emotions have definite survival value in a primitive environment of Darwinian competition. The problem is what happens when we react emotionally to complex situations which can best be solved through reason and scientific method?

Emotions still have survival value in the modern world. This is particularly true for young children who do not yet have enough knowledge to cope with situations logically and scientifically, let alone in terms of objective ethics. For a young child to react fearfully to strangers, for example, is perfectly normal and probably has survival value in a society replete with psychopaths. However, as the normal child matures he eventually learns to react to strangers with cautious friendliness as a means of increasing his own ability to predict and control. Similarly, we intuitively believe that the behavioral responses of young children, who are almost entirely guided by emotions, are inapprorpriate for adults. In general, when adults display the same emotional responses as children, we consider them neurotic, or even psychotic in some cases, for example, when they throw homicidal temper tantrums. Therefore, it is intuitively accepted that part of the process of maturing involves substituting logic and reason for emotion in our behavior. Although we may intuitively accept the notion that a normal mature adult is less emotional than a normal young child, it is not so obvious that the more ethical adults are less emotional than the less ethical adults. Other things being equal, i.e., the organic predisposition to emotionalism, it is not at all obvious that emotionalism in adults may be a consequence of ethical immaturity. However, we will show that neurotic emotionalism is unavoidable for unethical persons. In general, the more unethical a person becomes, the more emotional and neurotic he becomes, until he is as destructively emotional as a young child, but without the compensating creative emotions of love, which all young children have as a consequence of being ethical. Furthermore, emotionalism in adults can be much more destructive than in children, because adults are more intelligent and have more power.

To react contrary to genetic, emotional programming is impossible for unethical persons. This is the case because (1) unethical persons value happiness above truth and (2) the satisfaction of emotions always makes persons happy at least temporarily. Emotionally determined desires are the strongest in the unethical person, and their satisfaction brings him the greatest happiness. In other words, he will satisfy his emotions first and expand truth second. When there is a conflict, he will sacrifice objective truth for happiness. However, because as long as an unethical person has not yet become immoral, he also has a need to expand truth, he will fulfill this need through ideology, psychofraud, and subjective truths which are emotionally satisfying. The more illusionary information he incorporates into his mind, i.e., the more neurotic he becomes, the more he must continue to support his illusions with new illusory subjective truths which in turn make him even more neurotic. Eventually the unethical neurotic creates a wall of psychofraud and emotion around all his illusions and completely blinds himself to objective truth. This state can be maintained by (1) remaining ignorant of almost all of science and the scientific method, and (2) by specializing in a field that is so narrow that he never has to relate it to the rest of the world. The ethical person, on the other hand, will thwart his emotions and abandon his illusions when they conflict with objective truth. In this way he grows in objective truth and in the process becomes less emotional and happier. An ethical person can be made unethical only when he is exposed to a destructive, unethical environment in which his search for truth is continuously punished and/or never rewarded. This always happens in totalitarian states but also occurs subtly in democracies (50).

Neither emotions nor happiness are inherently unethical, and each has a role to play in the evolutionary process, both for individuals and for the species. It is only when emotions and happiness are the criteria by which decisions are made that persons and societies become unethical. Happiness and emotions are not the proper criteria for organizing a progressive society or building a healthy and creative life.

The preprogrammed interpretation of a situation is almost completely replaced by learned interpretations in human beings, but the emotional responses, once a situation is interpreted as aggressive, fearful or loving, may still be largely determined by biological programming. Sometimes this programming is only indirectly genetic, e.g., when emotional responses are determined by hormones.

Through the proper administration of hormones to all mammals, including humans, it is possible to completely reverse sexual desires (126). A female rat treated with male hormones shortly after or before birth will develop secondary male characteristics and when mature, will interpret females in estrus as a loving situation and will try to copulate with them. At the same time it will regard male competitors for the females aggressively and it will fight with them. Therefore, a single injection of hormones at a critical time can completely reverse some of the normal emotions of animals for the rest of their lives (162). There is evidence that some human homosexuals might have been subjected to a similar abnormal influx of hormones into their system during gestation because of genetically or environmentally determined hormone imbalances in the fetus or mother (37, 126). The result is that emotions related to the sex drive have become reversed. Homosexuals may be loving and aggressive in ways typical of their opposite sex. In our society, homosexuals have therefore more of an emotional handicap to overcome in ethical development than do heterosexuals; but they have the ethical and moral potential of all persons. The behaviorists as well as some Freudians believe that sexual response is entirely learned. However, the scientific findings given above contradict this.

This does not mean that any mammal cannot be taught to behave homosexually or heterosexually by extreme conditioning techniques. What it means is that sexual behavior is more determined by biological than by the psychosocial programming in almost all naturally occurring cases. When any organism, raised within the normal environmental range of its species, behaves in such a way that when it is given a free choice of mating with its own sex or with the opposite sex, more often than not chooses its own sex, then we say that organism is homosexual. If it chooses the opposite sex, then the organism is heterosexual.

The emotional reaction of many human beings to a complex, scientific society is very much like that of animals who have had their sexually related emotions reversed. Just as an artificially induced hormonal environment of the opposite sex can reverse sexual behavior, so can the artificially induced mechanistic environment of technological society induce behavior appropriate to a more primitive society. Our emotional responses are dependent on how we have learned to interpret a situation. When a situation is potentially dangerous, uncontrollable and unpredictable, a normal response is to react fearfully. As society becomes more complex and dangerous through technology and its misuses, people react fearfully and either flee from it into psychofraud or surrender to it through bureaucracy (50). The net effect is that they do not cope with the real problems, but only satisfy their emotional needs.

Probably the strongest emotional need is that for security, i.e., the absence of aggression or potential aggression.* This is derived from our basic need to survive and is in accordance with Maslow's intuitive notions about the hierarchy of needs. Human beings learned early, through genetic and environmental programming, that any power which could not be predicted and controlled was potentially dangerous and resulted in insecurity. Therefore, human beings have an emotional need to predict and control all perceived forces of nature, i.e., to be secure. This represents the shackling or imprisonment, i.e., complete control, of a potential aggressor.

On an emotional level this need can be satisfied by psychofraud. However, science and technology have created a world so complex and dangerous that to attempt to deal with it through psychofraud, while gaining temporary emotional satisfaction, will quickly bring about the ultimate reality of death. Although the psychofraud of sympathetic magic may have given man considerable emotional satisfaction and caused little damage in a primitive environment, to use sympathetic magic or its modern equivalents of psychofraud for dealing with the realities of nuclear war, pollution and genetic decay can only prove disastrous. However, these problems are so complex and apparently beyond the power

* The concept of "aggression" in this context also includes aggression by nature in the form of floods, earthquakes, and other natural disasters, such as inadequate food supply. Security is a state of mind in which we believe we have or can readily obtain all we need and have no fear of losing what we already have.

of most people, that they are now turning to emotionally satisfying ways equivalent to sympathetic magic for dealing with these very real problems, viz. the growing interest in witchcraft and the Jesus movement (46). The psychofraud of neomysticism,* Marxism, psychotherapy and most so-called social sciences are the modern equivalents of sympathetic magic. They represent an emotional escape from reality.

The most unpredictable factor in the total environment of modern society is human behavior. It is the unpredictability and uncontrollability of human behavior, particularly that of the political leaders, which makes the fruits of modern science so dangerous. Therefore, any emotionally satisfying variety of psychofraud is accepted if it promises to predict and control human behavior. The fact that the practitioners of these psychofrauds obtain material and emotional security from their practices makes the psychofraud appear even more attractive to those who are seeking happiness, e.g., Arica, Transcendental Meditation, Scientology, and other forms of commercial mysticism. All men become complete victims of their emotions when they seek happiness. Only the desire for objective truth can make us transcend emotional determinism.

DETERMINISM

Man can sometimes do as he wills, but he can never will as he wills. Our desires are genetically programmed by nature and engendered by our environment. Our wishes, our needs, and our emotions are completely determined by our heredity and the circumstances of our life. The unanswered question throughout the ages has been, How can man control himself if he cannot control his emotions?

* *Neomysticism* refers to attempts to reconcile traditional mysticism and modern science, e.g., *Crack in the Cosmic Egg* by J. S. Pierce, and *The Center of the Cyclone* by J. C. Lilly. The "reconciliation" is made at the expense of objective truth.

The problem of determinism has never been adequately solved, and we are not going to do so now. However, we can do the next best thing which is to show how a person can become free from the tyranny of his own emotions. The act of freeing ourselves from emotional determinism is itself dependent on circumstances beyond our control. But once we have liberated ourselves from destructive emotion, then our lives can be governed by ethics and reason instead of by emotional whims. In the process, we will eliminate all neuroses.

As long as our basic goal is happiness we will be ruled by our emotions. As long as our basic goal is happiness, the net effect of our lives will be unhappiness. As long as our basic goal is happiness, we will feel compelled to satisfy our strongest emotions regardless of the consequences. One of the consequences will be that we will remain neurotic.

We have seen that the only basic desire which can be successfully substituted for happiness is the desire for objective truth. Therefore, if we are to become free of emotional determinism, we must choose objective truth for ourselves and others as our *sole* goal. This is the most difficult choice that any human being will ever make, because our family, our friends, our teachers, our political leaders, our business associates, indeed our whole society may seem oriented entirely toward the basic goal of happiness. Therefore, how can this choice be made?

THE DIALECTIC OF CHOICE

Any choice we make is determined by our minds and our environment. Our minds are determined by our bodies, which in turn are determined by our heredity and our environment. Yet we constantly make choices and feel that they are *our* choices and that we have free will. From a metaphysical point of view, we know that free will is an illusion and that it may even be a self-contradicting concept. Still we make choices.

We as individuals cause events even though something originating outside ourselves may cause us to cause them. As knowledge, i.e., objective truth, expands, so does the ability to predict and control events, e.g., the scientific revolution of the last 300 years. By increasing our knowledge, we have greatly increased our ability to predict and control the physical, biological and, to a lesser extent, the psychosocial environments. Extrapolating this process to infinity, we see that if we had complete and total knowledge of everything in the universe, we should be able to predict and control everything, including ourselves. In other words, the mind would have become an effect of itself. Our thoughts would not be determined by things outside of ourselves because all things would be a part of us. This is the case because all existence represents information, and to incorporate all knowledge is to incorporate all information (50, 51).*

Of course, it may not be feasible to incorporate all knowledge into a single entity, particularly if the universe is infinite, as there is reason to believe that it might be (60, 61). However, our knowledge of objective truth can continue to grow forever. As our knowledge grows, so does our ability to predict and control. In the process we become "freer" because an ever increasing part of all the events in the universe is being caused by us.

Truth can make us free, but it is always a relative freedom. Complete freedom and the absence of all determinism is as impossible as complete, total, infinite knowledge. The choice is whether to grow in freedom and knowledge or to seek happiness.

* *Information* is used in the abstract mathematical sense of the word, the symbolic representation of events and relationships.

The act of increasing our knowledge is what enables us to make the choice. Just as a subhuman animal cannot choose objective truth above happiness, neither can an ignorant human being make this choice. What makes the choice of objective truth over happiness a practical reality is that knowledge can grow, although we have happiness as one of our basic goals.

Man has grown in knowledge not so much because he loved truth as because he could not be happy in a competitive environment while he was ignorant. Knowledge gave him power. Power gave him security and happiness. As his power grew, he became increasingly secure from all the vagaries of nature, save threats from his fellowman, who was also growing in knowledge and power. Man has continued to evolve primarily because of competition with his own kind. This has caused him to grow in knowledge and power, but it has also caused him to create the means of his own destruction, because his knowledge of the psychosocial environment has not kept pace with his knowledge of the physical and biological environment. Ethical man now has the knowledge to view himself in an evolutionary perspective and see that the pursuit of objective truth as his sole goal is the only means by which he can learn to predict and control himself. Man has the knowledge ethically to reprogram himself, if he has not become unethical by accepting happiness as the prime value of life. Today humanity must become ethical by deliberate choice or it will destroy itself through ethical decay.

The only common denominator in evolution is increasing intelligence through increasing complexity. This increase in complexity and intelligence has been the result of the haphazard process of evolution through random mutations and natural selection. However, the random mutations which led to the uniquely human property of man's having knowledge of his own knowledge decreased the random element in human evolution, since knowledge then could be accumulated through culture and not solely through changes in biological structure resulting from random genetic mutations.

The increase in knowledge led to an increase in intelligence and power, and so eventually human evolution became *primarily*, not entirely, a psychosocial process. In Julian Huxley's words, "Man has become evolution-conscious of itself." It is this ability to see himself in an evolutionary perspective which enables man to choose objective truth over happiness as his basic goal, if he has not become unethical.

The desire for happiness is programmed into the human nervous system. This is evidenced by the reinforcing properties of all pleasurable sensations in young children. Less obvious is the fact that a desire for truth is also programmed into our nervous system. This is the source of the Moral Sense. It is evidenced by the fact that almost all children learn and grow ethically and by the cultural evolution of the human species. While man existed in the primitive Darwinian competition of prehistory, there was no conflict between his desires for happiness and truth since he could not remain happy unless he grew in knowledge. Modern society, in eliminating all vestiges of Darwinian competition through socialism, has made it possible for all men to be happy through psychofraud.

Psychofraud fulfills man's needs for happiness as well as his need for truth, since we need only *believe* that we have truth in order to fulfill our need for it and, as a consequence, be happy. However, it is in the nature of psychofraud that in a rapidly changing world our illusions of truth cannot for long be maintained unless we blind ourselves to objective reality. In the democracies, persons are now blinding themselves to reality with the psychofrauds of mysticism, drugs, psychotherapy, social "science," and other alleged ways of "expanding their minds." In the communist states the entrenched bureaucracies maintain their own psychofraud through the brutal suppression of all dissent and criticism of the official ideology. If entropy does not destroy this generation, it will almost certainly destroy future generations, unless we, as a species, deliberately incorporate objective ethical principles.

The pattern of human evolution is that we are tending toward a single, united planetary species. Currently it matters little whether it is a communistic or democratic system of government which prevails, since both systems are (1) socialistic, (2) permeated with psychofraud, and (3) sufficiently developed technologically to create a completely automated society where all persons may continue to reproduce for centuries while living in a state of complete psychofraud. Both systems are entropic.

The last vestige of evolutionary competition is that remaining between the great power blocs. Through assimilation or annihilation, eventually one system—Soviet, Maoist, socialist, ethnocentric (e.g., Japan or a United Europe), etc.—will emerge as the sole government of the earth. If the basic choice between happiness and truth has not been made by then, the human race will decay genetically, because once all competition is eliminated, it will then be possible in a totally automated society for all persons to grow in happiness and reproduce without growing in knowledge (50). This destruction of the ability to perceive objective reality is the antithesis of natural selection; it has meant extinction for thousands of species in the past.

The only reasons for choosing objective truth over happiness as our sole goal are that (1) we perceive ourselves as part of a cosmic process in which knowledge and intelligence have been growing for billions of years and can continue to grow for billions of years more and perhaps forever (50), and (2) only the constant deliberate pursuit of objective truth for ourselves and others can maximize the happiness of the human race. However, in the latter case it is a happiness which comes about indirectly from leading a purposeful life. To a moral person, joy is the trivial consequence of pursuing truth; it is not a basic goal.

The dialectic is between happiness and truth. The choice between the two can only be made by seeing man in an evolutionary perspective. We have the knowledge to make the choice. Only ethical persons who have the intelligence and the opportunity to acquire the knowledge *will* make the choice. The choice of objective truth as our sole basic goal is the foundation of Ethical Therapy, but this choice can only be made by those who have not been conditioned to desire happiness above truth. The choice can only be made by persons who have remained ethical.

THE THRESHOLD OF MORALITY

Ethical Therapy is not a universal therapy. It can never work on persons who are unethical, because circumstances beyond their control already forced them to make the wrong choice. Unethical persons will seek to increase their happiness through psychofraud, and they will be impervious to Ethical Therapy, because objective truth will more often than not make them unhappy by making them aware of their own illusions and inadequacies.

Ethical Therapy is only for persons who through fortunate heredity and environment have the intelligence and the inclination to value truth above happiness. These persons are at a threshold of morality. Ethical Therapy can help them cross this threshold. At the threshold is the deliberate choice of objective truth as our sole basic goal.

A behaviorist would say that we need only reward persons suitably whenever they increase knowledge for themselves and others, to achieve our purpose of having those persons constantly expanding the collective ability of the human race to predict and control its total environment. This, however, would only take persons to the threshold of morality; it would not take them beyond it. The threshold of morality can only be crossed by deliberate choice—an ethical quantum jump.

A person who has been conditioned by punishment and/or reward to value and seek truth still has happiness as a basic goal. If the reinforcement is changed so that the pursuit of truth causes pain and brings no pleasure, then ethics can be extinguished as can any other kind of behavior. To cross the threshold of morality is to make a deliberate choice, without coercion or extraneous rewards, to pursue truth as an end in itself and not as a means to an end. To cross the threshold is to develop a state of mind where no pain is greater than the destruction of truth and no joy is greater than the expansion of truth. That this state of mind can be developed is evidenced by the existence of the great moral leaders of history previously mentioned and the many lesser spiritual heroes who preferred to die rather than to live a lie (20, 30, 32, 82, 99, 101, 143).

The crossing of the threshold of morality can be aided by persons who have themselves (1) already crossed it or (2) are close to it; but the final choice is ultimately made alone by each person who crosses. Those who cross have become moral. Those who stand before the threshold are ethical. Ethical persons in general and moral persons in particular may guide us and point the way, but we must take the final step by ourselves. Furthermore, we can never be sure that we have actually crossed the threshold. We will always have doubts that some unbearable pain to ourselves or our loved ones might make us renounce truth for happiness. What happens once the threshold is crossed is that our confidence in our own ethics grows and all our destructive emotions completely vanish. We become devoid of aggression and fear. If we should ever feel these emotions, then we know that we have not yet crossed the threshold. If we ever feel the slightest twinge of anger or anxiety, then we know that we have not crossed the threshold of morality. It is clear that aggression and fear can be destructive, but what of love?

LOVE

Love is a state of mind where the welfare of another person is sufficiently important to us that we are willing to sacrifice some of our welfare for his. To ethical persons in general and moral persons in particular, "welfare" refers solely to the ability to predict and control the total environment now and in the future, since this is the only objective criterion for truth. Theirs is an ethical love. To unethical persons in general and immoral persons in particular welfare is synonymous with happiness. Theirs is a perverse love.

To an unethical person, the greatest good is that which makes for the greatest happiness. Deceit is countenanced if it makes persons happy. The killing of ideological heretics and the suppression of error, i.e., opinions contrary to the established ideology, is countenanced if it brings the masses closer to heavenly happiness, whether it is the supernatural Christian heaven of disembodied souls or the materialistic, worldly heaven of a communist utopia. When unethical persons "love," they will readily sacrifice truth for the happiness of those they "love."

An ethical person finds it difficult and a moral person, impossible to sacrifice truth for anyone's happiness, including his own. An ethical love is, therefore, not a love of passion, but a love of reason. It is similar in concept to the Greek agape or the traditional Christian concept of "love." It does not include the Greek eros or physical love, although sex itself can be ethical. Ethical love gives without seeking to take; it is nonpossessive.

Ethical love increases truth by increasing the knowledge and intelligence of others. To cause physical harm to anyone is to decrease his intelligence, i.e., ability to predict and control his environment. Similarly, to teach, cure, nurture and prevent injury is to increase, or at least maintain intelligence. To engage in mutually voluntary sexual contact is to increase intelligence by increasing knowledge of ourselves in others and knowledge of others in ourselves. The biblical euphemism of "knowing" is most appropriate. To create and nurture ethical, healthy, new human life is clearly a way of expanding truth. Therefore, sex when it results from mutual ethical love is ethical. Conversely, rape, prostitution and other forms of sex without ethical love at best only increase happiness and do nothing to expand truth. Sex without ethical love is perversion.

Love can be a preprogrammed pattern of behavior, i.e., an emotion, which begins as a compulsion to behave in such a way that the welfare of others is enhanced. This is most clearly seen in the instinctual maternal love of most female birds and mammals for their offspring. From an evolutionary point of view, this instinctual love helped the species survive, because it usually manifested itself by the nurture and protection of the young. In some higher species, e.g., emus and wolves, love was extended to include the mate as well as the offspring. In the highest mammalian species, e.g., primates, love was sometimes extended to include an entire family or clan. In all these cases, love increased the intelligence of the species. We note that love is virtually nonexistent in species of the reptilian or lower levels of evolution. It is, therefore, a relatively recent programming of the nervous system through genetic mutation and natural selection.

Love is what enabled man to survive as a group and expand knowledge and intelligence through group effort that was beyond the capability of any individual. Love is therefore central to human evolution and to the expansion of truth. The problem is that emotional love is easily perverted by unethical persons and societies so that welfare becomes synonymous with happiness. When this happens, ethical love dies. Perverse love is closely tied to the other basic emotions and is equally destructive. Ethical love is a cool and rational state of mind which is not tied to the other emotions.

When a person becomes moral, he is devoid of perverse love but filled with ethical love which manifests itself in his conscious, deliberate desire to increase the intelligence of other ethical persons even at great cost and discomfort to himself. Only moral persons will die so that truth will live on in persons they have never met. Ethical love is a state of mind which crosses the threshold of morality. But it persists as an unemotional, purified state, completely under rational control. Ethical love is not uncontrolled emotion; it is an energizing force in moral persons, but it is not their master. Only perverse love is uncontrollable. Moral persons are devoid of perverse love and all other emotions.

Therefore, all emotions disappear in moral persons. The ethical love which remains is not, properly speaking, emotion, because it is not preprogrammed, but a result of a rational choice deliberately made when crossing the threshold of morality. It is the goal of Ethical Therapy to make persons moral, not to eliminate emotion. The elimination of emotion is merely a side effect of becoming moral and valuing nothing but objective truth.

To be devoid of emotion is not to be devoid of human warmth, feeling or sensitivity. It merely means that our actions are rationally determined and are not programmed by the primitive portions of the brain. One can be completely devoid of emotions and still be capable of joy, happiness, and affection. Indeed, the greatest happiness comes from leading an ethical and purposeful life. But to a moral person happiness is trivial. Similarly, only an ethical person shows true unpossessive love and affection.

We cannot avoid all destructive emotions in particular without avoiding all emotions in general. However, the elimination of all emotion will enhance creativity, not decrease it. When we lose our emotions through ethical development, we merely lose a way of being happy, as well as a way of being unhappy, as is evidenced in young children maturing. Persons are neurotically attached to their emotions only because of an evolutionarily obsolete need to be happy. They cannot conceive of happiness without emotions. The irony is that true, lasting happiness and joy come from becoming moral, and becoming moral implies the elimination of all emotion. We eliminate emotions not by directly choosing to do so, but by deliberately pursuing objective truth.

Ethical Therapy involves no more than helping persons cross the threshold of morality by deliberately choosing objective truth as their sole goal. They need not even consider emotion. It is a painless process. A person must cross the threshold by himself, but others can help him determine (1) whether he is approaching the threshold and (2) whether he has in fact crossed. We must each be our own pilot across the threshold, but through ethical love we can get help in navigation.

NAVIGATION

Navigation is the science of knowing at all times where we are, relative to where we want to be. In crossing the threshold of morality, we must know at all times whether our actions are ethical or unethical. That is to say, we must know whether our behavior is increasing or decreasing objective truth. Without a navigator to help us, we can lose our way and succumb to psychofraud and the belief that we are expanding truth, when in fact we are only expanding illusions and destroying truth.

Man's competition against the forces of nature, animals and his own kind has been an invaluable aid in helping him find his way toward the threshold of morality. The human losers in the competition were usually more prone to psychofraud than the winners, viz., the triumph of Protestantism over Catholicism, the triumph of Europe over Islam, the triumph of materialistic, rational Western Civilization over the mystical civilizations of the East (50). So long as competition was maintained, mankind had a built-in navigator guiding his evolution. However, the competition is now about to end either through annihilation or the hegemony of one sociopolitical system over all nations. Furthermore, the trend in all the existing systems is to eliminate all forms of internal and external competition. Competition is eliminated by monolithic bureaucracies with monopolies of function. This is the case in both so-called communistic and capitalistic societies. Internal competition is eliminated by psychofraud.

Human competition is seen as something evil and destructive by many of the thoughtful young.* Clearly competition only makes some of the victors happy. It never makes the losers happy, and in a Darwinian setting, almost all lose. So long as happiness is a basic goal, competition cannot be justified, and man will seek to destroy his only means of navigation. The only way to solve the dilemma is to change the nature of the competition.

CREATIVE COMPETITION

Creative competition is a necessary process for navigating and crossing the threshold of morality. All competition has a creative element, but Darwinian competition also has what may appear to be destructive elements, since Darwinian competition leads to the extinction of a life-form or a whole class of life-forms. However, in the broader context of the total information, knowledge and intelligence of the biomass, the net effect of Darwinian competition is creative; it decreases entropy.

In order to navigate to and through the threshold of morality, we must apply creative Darwinian competition to our own thoughts so that thoughts which are true grow and

* See the "underground press" in general and *Rolling Stone* in particular. This view is most aptly summarized in the anti-rationalistic tract, *The Greening of America,* by Charles Reich.

multiply and thoughts which are false perish. We must do this collectively as a society and as individuals. The social aspects of creative competition are presented elsewhere (50). Here we will only discuss the individual aspects of creative competition.

Each thought we have represents a subjective model of some aspect of nature. Insofar as our thoughts bear a true relationship to objective reality, they will enable us to predict and control that aspect of nature of which they are a model. Because no part of nature exists completely independently of any other part and nature is itself infinite in either a real or a practical sense, our models of nature will always be incomplete and lead to errors in our efforts to predict and control. When these errors are tied to emotions, we say that a person is "neurotic." When these errors are of a purely factual or logical nature, we say that the person is "lacking intelligence." By purely scientific means we can continuously reduce the errors which result from a lack of intelligence, although we can never eliminate them entirely. With Ethical Therapy we can eliminate *all* the errors which result from neuroses.

Our neurotic thoughts are those thoughts we cherish solely because they make us happy. Objective reality has no bearing on neurotic thoughts once they have been engendered. Indeed, when neurotic thoughts conflict with those which are in accordance with objective reality, a common practice is to reject reality and hold on to the neurotic thoughts. If this is done systematically on a grand scale, then we say the person is "psychotic." Our neurotic thoughts are therefore in constant competition with our true thoughts. Creative competition in thought means that our neurotic thoughts perish and our true thoughts grow and multiply.

Since neurotic thoughts are maintained only as means of being happy, the elimination of happiness as a basic goal will eliminate all neurotic thoughts. Once neurotic thoughts have been eliminated, competition between thoughts can be entirely creative. Natural selection will eliminate thoughts which are in conflict with other thoughts which better enable us to predict and control objective reality. The question is how do we first begin to eliminate neurotic thoughts?

ENDING NEUROSES

If the behaviorists were correct in assuming that all behavior results entirely from operant conditioning through reward and punishment, then there would be no hope of producing moral persons and completely eliminating neuroses. This would be the case because persons would be unable to transcend the pleasure principle. The fact that throughout the ages there have been moral persons who were willing to stand entirely alone and suffer ignominy, torture, and death for the sake of truth disproves the basic behaviorist contention.

Morality cannot be extinguished. Ethics can be extinguished only in people who are not yet moral. The facts that (1) moral persons are very rare and (2) the vast majority of mankind apparently has never gone beyond the pleasure principle, indicate that there is a great deal of truth to the behaviorist model and that conditioning techniques can shape much of human behavior and probably all animal behavior.

Through simple techniques of reward and punishment, but mostly through proper rewards (137, 138), we can end many neurotic patterns of behavior such as phobias, compulsive smoking and drinking, bed-wetting and even some sexual aberrations (77, 111, 118, 170, 171). However, the vast majority of persons go to psychotherapists not for these more straightforward and clear-cut problems, but because they are unhappy (42, 43, 28, 71, 146). As noted earlier, they need a friend, even a paid friend (129). It is a feeling of generalized anxiety and depression, or more aptly, "demoralization," which is the overwhelming symptom of neurotics (42, 43,

71). It is these generalized, nonbehaviorial, emotional states which impede their productivity and creativity. Behaviorism does not even recognize these or any other mental states. It can only treat clear-cut behavioral disorders with clear-cut symptoms. However, psychofraud thrives on these vague emotional disorders. Psychofraud can and sometimes does bring emotional peace and happiness. Ethical Therapy can do the same.

Psychofraud relieves anxiety through self-delusion; it is the thought that he understands the source of his emotions which makes them tractable to the neurotic. However, the psychofraudulent mode of therapy is not aimed at increasing creativity or making persons moral. It does not take persons beyond the pleasure principle. It does not, nor does it seek to, eliminate emotions. Indeed, most forms of psychofraud celebrate emotions and seek merely to help their patients give full vent to them and express them more freely (65, 66, 74, 89, 132, 179). However, any victim of psychofraud will have his equanimity collapse as soon as his illusions come into unavoidable conflict with reality. For this reason psychotherapists and their patients have a suicide rate which is more than 50 times that of the general population (40, 47, 48, 158, 178). For this reason, it appears that psychotherapists are among the most neurotic members of society and do themselves require constant "therapeutic" treatment to reinforce their psychofraud (24, 47, 81, 115).

Ethical Therapy involves using simple conditioning techniques and suggestion to eliminate simple bad habits and create simple good ones. In this respect there is a wide overlap among behavior therapy, hypnotherapy, and Ethical Therapy. Ethical Therapy also seeks to provide ethical friendship as does classical therapy. *What is unique to Ethical Therapy is that it seeks to eliminate anxiety and all destructive emotions indirectly by reorienting the person's value system toward the sole value of objective truth.* This can be done in the following ways:

1. The person must realize that much of his behavior, as currently manifested, has no other objective than to make him happy.
2. The person must then realize that the desire for truth is inherent to him and is as much a part of his nature as his desire for happiness.
3. The person must then learn to see himself in an evolutionary perspective where the only common denominator to all of evolution is increasing intelligence through increasing complexity and information.
4. The person must then see that the pursuit of happiness is a frustrating and self-defeating goal which can only lead to unhappiness.
5. The person must then deliberately and consciously begin to make decisions on the basis of what maximizes truth and not on the basis of what maximizes happiness.
6. Once the decisions of his everyday life begin to have a conscious ethical basis, the person will begin to feel a relaxation of anxiety because he now has an objective way of making decisions and he need no longer have emotional conflicts, since objective truth is independent of his emotions.
7. The application of ethical principles to his everyday decisions will bring him closer to the threshold of morality until he crosses it through an act of will, the ethical quantum jump.
8. The main role of the Ethical Therapist is to be a navigator and help the person analyze his decisions in the light of objective truth by seeing if these decisions are violating ethical principles.

ETHICAL PRINCIPLES

Given that the prime ethic is

Each person must do his best to maximize objective truth

then a personal ethical code is logically derivable from this ethic. For example, it follows immediately that lying, for any purpose, is always unethical, since it diminishes objective truth. However, it does not logically follow that we must tell the truth to everyone. We must never lie, but we should speak the truth only to ethical persons who themselves seek to expand objective truth and will use the information we give them for that purpose. To persons we deem unethical or engaged in unethical purposes, we should speak neither lies nor truth, but remain uncommunicative. For example, it is unethical to tell a potential murderer where his intended victim is hiding, but it is also unethical to lie to him. We should remain uncommunicative, even if it costs us our lives. By giving false information we always diminish truth. By giving true information to unethical persons we increase their intelligence and ability to destroy truth. This is why unethical persons should be avoided. We must never cooperate in any way with evil.

A heuristic, nonrigorous, but detailed derivation of ethical principles is given elsewhere (50). A completely rigorous derivation of ethical principles is beyond the scope of a popular book (51). Here we will merely state the basic principles which follow from the prime ethic and then show how to apply them. They are as follows:

1. Only actions which increase objective truth are ethical.
2. Any action which decreases objective truth for any person is unethical.
3. Unethical means can never achieve ethical ends.
4. Means which are not ends are never ethical.
5. It is unethical to tolerate unethical behavior.
6. It is unethical to be certain.
7. It is ethical to doubt.
8. Inaction is unethical.

Now we will consider these principles one by one to see what they mean and then give examples of their use.

First Principle: Only actions which increase objective truth are ethical.

Clearly the first principle follows directly from the prime ethic, since if we waste energy and resources on activities which do not expand knowledge and intelligence, we are not maximizing objective truth. Any action which neither increases nor decreases truth is merely trivial, but it is unethical to waste resources on trivial activity, since by definition trivial activity can do no more than increase happiness. The more resources, including parts of our life, we waste, the less capable we are of expanding truth.

To learn, to teach and to create are the only bases of ethical behavior. To communicate objective or subjective truth to any ethical person is always ethical because this increases the collective ability of the human race to predict and control the total environment. To nurture and heal ethical persons is ethical because this expands or maintains their intelligence. In short, to be loving with any ethical person is always ethical.

Second Principle: Any action which decreases objective truth for any person is unethical.

It is always unethical to diminish truth for any person, because we can never increase truth by diminishing it. Because all of nature is an interconnected whole, to degrade any part of it is to degrade all of it. Because we are an interdependent species, to diminish truth for any person is to diminish it for all persons. Therefore, it is clearly unethical to lie to or to maliciously hurt any person in any way. It is also unethical to increase the intelligence of unethical persons, because this will increase their power to destroy and will lead to a decrease in objective truth.

Third Principle: Unethical means can never achieve ethical ends.

It follows immediately from the first and the second principles that unethical means can never achieve ethical ends. This is the case because only the expansion of truth is ethical, and any unethical means will necessitate the destruction of truth. As in the second principle, we cannot expand truth by diminishing it. Therefore, it is unethical to lie to or maliciously hurt a single ethical person, even if we feel it might save our lives or the lives of the entire human race. To deliberately destroy or in any way diminish a single innocent, ethical life for the alleged welfare of any group, no matter how large and progressive, is always unethical. In the long run, it must diminish the welfare of the group it was supposed to help.

It follows immediately that slavery or any form of involuntary servitude, such as the draft system, is an absolute wrong which can never be justified, because to diminish any person's freedom is to diminish him as a human being and to diminish truth. A historical example of unethical means bringing about unethical ends in the long run is in the institution of chattel slavery in the southern United States. The greatest harm done by slavery was not to the slaves, who were still abundantly harmed, but to the masters and their progeny, who were supposed to be the main beneficiaries of slavery; i.e., their awareness was supposed to be increased as was the awareness of the slaves who supposedly were saved from a life of savagery and brought the fruits of Christianity and Western Civilization. The damage of the Civil War alone was greater than any economic benefit that the masters ever obtained from slavery. The damage of a segregated, insular society produced as the aftermath of slavery has impeded the intellectual, cultural and industrial development of the South to this very day. The political turmoil, social chaos and anguish brought about by the attempts to correct the lingering effects of slavery, e.g., segregation, is the most divisive and destructive force in American society. The Americans of today are still paying and will continue to pay for the ethical mistakes of their ancestors, who used unethical means to achieve what they thought to be ethical ends. In an evolutionary perspective, the sins of the fathers are always visited upon their progeny even unto the tenth generation.

History is replete with many similar examples of unethical means never achieving ethical ends, the most recent one being the disaster of the American Indo-China war where the attempt to support one corrupt, military dictatorship against another led to the most divisive, destructive and costly war experienced by the Americans since their Civil War. Unethical means can never achieve ethical ends for society or the individual.

Fourth Principle: Means which are not ends are never ethical.

This principle follows directly from the third principle. Since the only ethical end is to expand truth, and unethical means can never expand truth, a means which is not an end is any means which does not expand truth. Such means are at best trivial and at worst unethical. Therefore, if our means are to be ethical, they must be ethical ends in themselves and not merely expedient means to an end. Trivial means can at best only bring about trivial results. As was shown previously, unethical means only bring about unethical results.

An example of a means which is not an ethical end but which becomes the central goal for most of mankind is the accumulation of wealth and power. Many thoughtful and ethical persons claim that riches are not their ultimate goal, but only a temporary means so that they can then have the wealth and the power to do what they want. However, it is inherent in human nature that, through a process of conditioning, the means—whether they are ethical, unethical or trivial—invariably become the ends. Therefore, persons who seek to maximize their wealth invariably become so obsessed with making money that before they know it their lives are over and all they have to show for it is a lot of money, which more often than not corrupts and destroys their children by taking away their opportunity to compete.

We see trivial and unethical means becoming ultimate ends among religious groups which practice ritualistic behavior until the ritual becomes the most important part of their lives and they cease to expand truth for themselves or others, e.g., dietary laws.

Only means which expand objective truth are ethical. Only the expansion of truth can be both the means and the end of ethical persons.

Fifth Principle: It is unethical to tolerate unethical behavior.

It is unethical to tolerate unethical behavior, because to tolerate it is to allow truth to be diminished. The prime ethic is that we must maximize truth. If we are to maximize truth, we must be creative and prevent destruction. It follows from the second law of thermodynamics that merely not preventing destruction is sufficient for everything in a closed system to be destroyed. For all practical purposes, human society is currently a closed system, little influenced by forces outside the solar system. If we tolerate destructive behavior among us, we will ourselves be destroyed and we will have failed to maximize truth. Therefore, it is unethical to tolerate unethical behavior.

If we passively allow ourselves to be deceived or injured, we are tolerating unethical behavior and being unethical. Therefore, we are ethically bound to defend ourselves against unethical persons. Only an unethical person would seek to destroy, and it is ethical to eliminate any destructive force. We can never be certain who is ethical, but the probabilities are such that if (1) we are ethical and (2) we are doing our best to behave ethically and (3) someone deliberately tries to deceive us or injure us, then that person is unethical. For reasons previously given, we should avoid unethical persons even if the only way to avoid them is by force. For example, if someone is trying to murder us, then we should use force to defend ourselves even to the point of causing severe or permanent harm to our aggressor. In so doing we are being ethical by eliminating a destructive force from our midst which would eventually probably destroy more than merely ourselves. However, the use of force is only justified when we are in imminent peril and are ourselves being subjected to unethical force. Because we can never be certain, we must engage in passive avoidance of unethical persons whenever possible and use force only as a last resort to protect our own intelligence and that of other ethical persons. The critical point is that we are never certain.

Sixth Principle: It is unethical to be certain.

It is unethical to be certain because it is objectively false to presume that we have complete information on any subject. Since everything in the universe is interrelated and we have only a small amount of information on any subject, we are always subject to errors. We objectively know that this is the case because we always make errors, however small, in all our attempts at precise prediction and control of nature. That part of the environment about which we make the most errors is the psychosocial, i.e., human behavior. Therefore, we must be most skeptical about any models which purport to predict and control human behavior, including Ethical Therapy, because (1) these models are almost never objectively tested and (2) when they are tested, they *always* have a great deal of error.

Because it is unethical to be certain, it is unethical to kill, injure or imprison human beings simply because our model tells us that they are unethical and that the net effect of their lives will be to decrease truth. If we believe that this is the case, we should avoid such persons and exile them from our midst when they have shown a systematic pattern of decreasing other persons' ability to predict and control (50). It is only when we feel almost certain that we or someone else is about to be forcefully, imminently and deliberately injured by an unethical person that force is justified. Even then, we must realize that we might be making a mistake in that truth may be destroyed for another in our attempt to preserve truth for ourselves. We must never lose all doubt.

Seventh Principle: It is ethical to doubt.

It is ethical to doubt, because we can only learn when we have doubts. Once a person has no doubts about any subject, that person has ceased to learn about that subject. All actions are either ethical, unethical or trivial. Since it is unethical to be certain, it is either trivial or ethical to doubt. Since learning is always ethical, doubting is always ethical and never trivial.

Persons only succumb to psychofraud when they lose their doubts. The Inquisition would not have burned heretics and the Nazis would not have massacred Jews if they had any doubts about their respective kinds of psychofraud. It is only when doubt is destroyed that truth is destroyed.

It was because Einstein doubted the sufficiency of the explanations of Newtonian mechanics that he created the theory of relativity. It is because Copernicus, Galileo, Kepler and finally Newton doubted the sufficiency of the Ptolomeic model of the universe that Newton created his general theory of gravitation. It was because the leaders of the Catholic Church had no doubts, that they burned Giordano Bruno and forced Galileo to recant. Doubt is the basis of truth. Systematic doubt is the basis of science. Science is the basis of all ethical action.

Eighth Principle: Inaction is unethical.

Inaction is unethical, because truth cannot be expanded passively. Truth is either forcefully expanded or it is destroyed by entropy (second law of thermodynamics). The old adage, It is only necessary for good men to do nothing in order for evil to triumph, is also derivable from objective ethical principles. We can neither expand truth nor eliminate unethical behavior without action. Therefore, inaction is not merely trivial, it is unethical. If no action is taken, truth will surely diminish. Since the prime ethic is that each person must do his best to expand truth, each person is individually responsible for taking ethical action.

The minimum action that must be taken is the expansion of truth for ourselves. No one can teach what he does not know. If we do not learn, we will never help others learn. However, a life devoted entirely to self-centered learning, while ethical, can never be moral. If we do not teach others what we have learned, truth will die with our lives and truth will not be maximized. We live on only in the truth we engender in others. The action of acquiring objective truth for ourselves will take us to the threshold of morality. But no one crosses the threshold who does not also act to expand truth for all mankind.

APPLYING ETHICAL PRINCIPLES

The eight ethical principles given in the previous section are the necessary navigation rules that each person needs in order to cross the threshold of morality. These principles are logically derivable (50, 51) from the single prime ethic,

Each person must do his best to maximize objective truth.

The prime ethic itself is not logically derivable. It is an ultimate basic goal; and such goals have no basis in logic, since they are ends in themselves and not means to any end. Logic can tell us whether our means are consistent with our ends, but it cannot tell us what our ends should be. However, logic can also tell us whether our ends are themselves consistent. In the previous chapter (50) we have seen that (1) happiness is a logically inconsistent end whose deliberate and exclusive pursuit can only lead to death, (2) mankind has only two basic goals, happiness and truth, and (3) the deliberate pursuit of objective truth as an end in itself will maximize both truth and happiness. Therefore, it is logical that humanity should choose objective truth as its sole goal irrespective of whether its basic objective is truth or happiness. However, the nature of man is such that if he has chosen happiness as his primary objective, he will delude himself with psychofraud and through emotion destroy his ability to logically cope with his own problems. This is neurosis, the epidemic disease of modern man, who has built a society on the foundation of psychofraud.

Although psychofraud is the foundation of modern society, the walls and all the superstructure are built by science. Science gives us our tools and power; but, for the majority of mankind, their reasons for existence, their guiding purposes and the basis for their happiness stem from psychofraud.

Ethical Therapy is a means for recasting the foundations of our society without destroying the superstructures. Ethical Therapy is a means which is an end. The specific techniques, e.g., ethical principles, may be in partial, logical error, but they cannot be in total error, because all the means are ends in themselves and all the same end—to expand objective truth as best we can. The very act of deliberately trying to expand objective truth will correct any errors in our means. The simple act of deliberately trying to expand objective truth as best we can will lead us to the threshold of morality and beyond, where all neuroses disappear and true joy is found in the infinite expansion of the human mind.

7

Ethical Perspective

For whosoever hath to him shall be given, and he shall have more abundance: but whosoever hath not, from him shall be taken away even that he hath.

Matthew 13:12

As has been shown, Ethical Therapy consists entirely in teaching persons to value objective truth above all things, including their own happiness. Ethical Therapy is not, properly speaking, psychotherapy, since its sole beneficiaries are those who are already healthier than the norm. It is a type of ethical transference. It will in no way help psychotics whose disease usually has an organic basis. It will in no way help the highly neurotic, who are that way only because they are unethical. The unethical can only become more unethical. Only ethical persons have the potential for creative growth.

Ethical Therapy is a way of making the healthy healthier and inoculating them permanently against all neuroses. If it is medicine, then it is preventive medicine. However, Ethical Therapy is related philosophically and practically to many of the traditional forms of psychotherapy. These relationships will now be discussed.

RELIGION AND ETHICAL THERAPY

Religion is the oldest form of psychotherapy and psychofraud. Religion and Ethical Therapy share the common goals of giving meaning and purpose to life. Ethical Therapy does it through the pursuit of the sole basic goal of objective truth. Religion does it through the pursuit of a goal of inner enlightenment through nonscientific means (nirvana, sanctifying grace, etc.), usually followed by a heavenly reward after death. Religion promises that the best of life comes after death. Ethical Therapy accepts only one life, since there is no scientific evidence for life after death, and in science all theories and hypotheses are assumed probably false until proven true. (See footnote on page 120.)

Ethical Therapy and religion each seek to create a unified model which explains everything in the universe. Ethical Therapy does it through science and the general theory of evolution (50, 51). Religion does it through revelation and theism.

Religion and Ethical Therapy share a common concern with the future of man and not just with the present. Both share the view that (1) man is more than the sum of his parts and that (2) there is something greater than man and man may eventually join with it, i.e., God and higher states of evolution for religion and Ethical Therapy, respectively (50).

Religion stresses faith. Ethical Therapy stresses doubt, i.e., scientific method and objective verifiability. Religion is based on man's emotional needs. Ethical Therapy is based on reason and the single, deliberately chosen rational goal of objective truth. Religion offers certainty and absolute truth. Ethical Therapy is relativistic and offers only probable truth.

Religion seeks to predict and control the environment through prayer; Ethical Therapy, through research and experimentation. The former stems from a reliance on supernatural authority, the latter from a reliance on science, technology, and objective verification. However, both religion and Ethical Therapy value artistic creativity. Ethical Therapy values any artistic expression which is not objectively harmful.

The incompatibility between religion and Ethical Therapy stems from the incompatibility between natural and supernatural goals. Religion stresses the immortality of the soul and that ultimate reality is beyond this life. The view of Ethical Therapy is that the soul, i.e., mind, probably dies with our bodies and that only the truth we engender in others survives our lives. Religion is concerned with the next world; Ethical Therapy, with this world. Religion is based on authority; Ethical Therapy rejects all authority not supported by scientific evidence.

CLASSICAL PSYCHOTHERAPY AND ETHICAL THERAPY

Classical Psychotherapy is any therapy which has been significantly influenced by the teaching of Freud. Classical Psychotherapy and Ethical Therapy share the following basic assumptions:

1. The existence of unconscious processes.
2. The fact that most and probably *all* complex human behavior is learned, although there may be some modulation by instinct.
3. Recognition of the emotional basis of most human behavior including neuroses.
4. Recognition of innate needs and instincts.

Classical and Ethical Therapy have the following contradictory assumptions and points of view:

Classical Psychotherapy	Ethical Therapy
1. Childhood events are of greatest importance in producing neuroses.	1. Neuroses can be produced at any age in persons who are not moral entirely by an accumulation of bad habits which lead to unethical, i.e., destructive behavior, which in turn leads to the orientation of one's life entirely toward the pursuit of happiness.
2. Environmental factors are of overwhelming importance in determining what is learned.	2. In our society, heredity is at least as important as environment in determining what is learned.
3. Human behavior can be understood from clinical observations of sick persons.	3. Human behavior can be understood only by controlled experimentation on healthy, as well as sick, persons.
4. A healthy person is one who can cope with life and does not engage in destructive behavior.	4. A healthy person is a creative person. Uncreative persons are never healthy. The healthier the person, the greater will be his ability to create.
5. A healthy person has and expresses the full range of human emotions.	5. In general, the healthier and more ethical a person is the less emotional he will be. A completely healthy person, i.e., a moral person, neither feels nor expresses any emotion other than ethical love, which in the strict sense of the word is not an emotion.

6. Ultimately all human decisions are based on irrational human needs.

6. Healthy, unneurotic persons base their decisions *entirely* on a logical, not necessarily correct, analysis of what will maximize objective truth. The emotional component is present only insofar as the person is neurotic.

Although classical psychotherapy and Ethical Therapy share certain common objectives, such as helping persons cope better with life in general and their emotions in particular, there are more incompatible than compatible goals between them. Classical psychotherapy seeks to make persons happy and well adjusted to their environment. Ethical Therapy is indifferent to any person's happiness and seeks to make all persons dissatisfied with their environment. Ethical Therapy seeks to inculcate the desire to be always changing the environment in such a way that objective truth is constantly growing at its maximum rate. One should never be satisfied with the rate at which truth is expanding. One must always be filled with creative dissatisfaction.

Classical psychotherapy assumes that there is no single unifying goal for mankind, but that each person will seek to pursue his own emotionally determined interests which may conflict with other persons' emotionally determined interests. Ethical Therapy considers total, infinite, objective truth as the sole goal compatible with human health and survival. Furthermore, there is never any conflict of interest between persons who pursue objective truth for themsleves and others as their sole goal. There are only differences in method, which can be resolved entirely by logic and science.

BEHAVIOR THERAPY AND ETHICAL THERAPY

Behaviorism is considered synonymous with Skinnerism. Psychologists such as Eysenck (38, 39), who use behavioral techniques but reject many of Skinner's theses, are not, properly speaking, behaviorists. Behavior therapy and Ethical Therapy share these common assumptions:

1. The purpose of behavioral science is to predict and control human behavior.
2. All behavior is learned.
3. At present, the only scientific knowledge we have about an organism, other than ourselves, is what can be objectively measured and observed.
4. Human behavior is modifiable by conditioning.

Behavior therapy and Ethical Therapy have the following contradictory assumptions and goals:

Behavior Therapy	**Ethical Therapy**
1. It is possible to develop a science of behavior *solely* by observing behavior. Introspection is valueless.	1. A science of behavior requires establishing relationships between behavior and all physical, biological and psychosocial processes. Introspection is valuable if it leads to an increasing ability to predict and control objective behavior.
2. There is no such thing as mind, since we cannot objectively measure or observe it. A science of behavior must be free of the concept of mind.	2. Mind is an effect of the body which we can each directly perceive in ourselves. Denying the existence of mind is worse than denying the existence of gravity because we cannot observe it but only its effects, i.e., the behavior of masses and not what causes that behavior. To develop a science of behavior without the concept of mind is worse than developing a science of dynamics without the concept of gravity. Further-

more, we know that we can modify our objective behavior by our subjective behavior of thinking. Thinking, a purely mental process, is probably our most important type of behavior. Ultimately there should be established a one-to-one correspondence between all mind states and brain states.

3. Since all behavior is learned, a person is entirely a product of his environment. In identical environments all persons would behave identically.

3. All behavior is learned, but the capacity to learn is largely inherited. Only persons who are biologically identical, i.e., identical twins, might behave identically in identical environments.

4. The full gamut of human potential exists within each person. Therefore, with the proper environment we can produce any type of human behavior in any person.

4. The full gamut of human potential does *not* exist within each person, although there may be a certain common denominator of behavior among all persons. High intelligence and great creative genius are primarily genetic phenomena. Therefore, although we may turn a congenital genius into an idiot, we probably cannot turn a congenital idiot into a genius.

5. Experiments with statistically matched groups are not necessary since our approach is such that we control all variables. Any behavioral changes must be due to our efforts.

5. We can never be sure that we have controlled all the variables. Therefore, we must do statistically controlled experiments.

6. Our only goal is to increase our ability to predict and control human behavior, not necessarily toward any particular end. "Give us the specifications and we will give you the person."

6. Our only goal is to increase the ability of the human race to predict and control its *total* environment—physical, biological and psychosocial. We wish to increase all persons' capability to create as individuals and to increase the total creativity of the human race without limit.

7. Although we do not have a specific goal for society, but rather only a method for achieving it, in general we wish to use conditioning techniques to create a happy, peaceful and well-adjusted community.

7. We are indifferent as to whether a society is happy, peaceful or well-adjusted. Our only concern is that objective truth is being maximized. A society in which objective truth is maximized may be the most peaceful and happy. However, this is merely a trivial biproduct of our basic goal. We do not wish to be well-adjusted in the sense of being satisfied with our place in life and the way things are organized. We want a society filled with creative tension and dissatisfaction with the status quo. We want a society evolving at its maximum possible rate and not smugly stagnating; such a society will produce an inner peace amidst the outer turmoil.

HUMANISTIC PSYCHOLOGY AND ETHICAL THERAPY

Humanistic psychology and Ethical Therapy share the following assumptions:

1. All behavior is natural in the sense that it is the product of natural laws.
2. Persons are born with certain innate needs which must be satisfied if the person is to become healthy, i.e., ethical.
3. All behavior results from an effort to satisfy certain needs.
4. We often are not conscious of what needs we are satisfying.
5. Although all of us have certain characteristics in common, each of us is unique and should be treated uniquely.
6. Needs common to all human beings at some time during their development are the needs for (a) security, (b) love, and (c) self-esteem.
7. The need for creativity (self-actualization) is the highest human need and will manifest itself only if the lower needs have been satisfied to some extent.

Humanistic psychology and Ethical Therapy are incompatible in the following assumptions and goals:

Humanistic Psychology	**Ethical Therapy**
1. A person is more than the net effect of his heredity and his environment. There is something in man which transcends nature.	1. A person is completely determined by his heredity and his *total* environment. The total environment includes all the natural forces in the universe and their interactive effects. Nothing transcends nature. All is a part of nature (50).
2. When the basic needs have been satisfied, a person will naturally and automatically gravitate toward the satisfac-	2. Although the satisfaction of basic needs is a necessary condition for ethical development, it is not a sufficient condition.

tion of the higher needs until he is self-actualizing.

If a person is not in an ethical environment, he can stagnate by concentrating on pleasurable activity which does not necessarily increase objective truth. This can occur without any outside coercion, because man has an infinite appetite for sensual pleasure. He must be given proper ethical guidance to go beyond the pleasure principle.

3. Since all neuroses are a product of some unsatisfied needs, we need only discover these needs and satisfy them in order to make a person healthy.

3. Neuroses may be produced by unsatisfied needs, but the most common cause is due to valuing happiness above truth. Therefore, merely satisfying needs will not eliminate neuroses and make a person ethical. Only ethical persons can engender ethics in one another and in themselves. Children are all born ethical but may become unethical if their unethical behavior is reinforced and their ethical behavior is not rewarded. This can occur through chance or through membership in an unethical social group or family.

4. The goal of humanistic psychology is to make persons self-actualizing so that they can do their own thing in their own way and not have anxieties about basic needs.

4. The goal of Ethical Therapy is to make persons desire the expansion of objective truth above all things. In so doing, persons will become self-actualizing and free of anxiety. However, these are side effects and not goals. It is possible to be self-actualizing and unethical, e.g., Hitler and Stalin. It is

possible to be devoid of anxiety and lack both ethics and self-actualization, e.g., lobotomized, tranquilized and otherwise drugged persons.

5. Although we value experimentation, we think that there is also much to be learned by clinical methods, insight, and subjectivity.

5. Only controlled experimentation can lead to constantly increasing understanding of nature and the expansion of objective truth. Any other approach is valid only insofar as it can be supported by controlled experiments.

UNIQUE FACTORS IN ETHICAL THERAPY

Ethical Therapy is unique in the following factors:

1. Objective truth is the sole goal.
2. Ethical Therapy is derived from an objective, scientific system of ethics, which is
   a. compatible with human nature,
   b. compatible with the basic evolutionary process and laws of nature,
   c. compatible with the basic ethical objectives of all major religions.
3. The emphasis is on a single goal and not on a particular method; this provides
   a. flexibility of method
   b. complete compatibility with scientific method.
4. Ethical Therapy is the only system which is truly universal in its applications and implications. For example:
   a. There are no conflicts possible between persons who pursue objective truth as a basic goal, contrasted with persons who pursue happiness as a basic goal, who will always have conflicts.
   b. Ethical Therapy is applicable to different sentient

species—the only possible common ethical system for the space age.

c. It is applicable through all time and space.
d. Ethical Therapy unifies all the social sciences in terms of a single, objective criterion (the growth in objective truth) which can be used as an indicator of progresses and optimality (50, 51).

PRACTICE

Any ethical person can practice Ethical Therapy by helping himself and others navigate to and through the threshold of morality. The more ethical and intelligent the practitioner, the more effective he or she will be in creating morality and ending neuroses. Because of the fundamental importance to Ethical Therapy of having a unified, evolutionary, ethical perspective of the universe, only persons with a broad, deep understanding of the physical, biological and psychosocial sciences are likely to be highly effective Ethical Therapists. Because Ethical Therapy is a form of education and not necessarily a medical treatment, persons seeking the help of an Ethical Therapist are regarded as students and not as patients.

The first obligation of the Ethical Therapist is to engender an evolutionary ethical perspective in his students. Toward this end he should serve as an educational counsellor helping his students acquire a thorough, integrated background in mathematics, physical science, biology, psychosocial science and their applications. The Science Education Extension and the Institute of Integrated Science exist for this purpose. Through these organizations, any ethical person, independently of his or her current ability, education or economic means, may acquire the intellectual and ethical background to become a fully creative scientific generalist.

At the same time that the student is learning integrated science, the Ethical Therapist can be helping him to (1) analyze his everyday actions in ethical terms, (2) see his emotional behavior and feelings as the consequence of his primitive need for happiness, and (3) increasingly value objective truth above happiness. In this way the Ethical Therapist is providing (1) ethical friendship, (2) emotional catharsis, (3) positive suggestion, and (4) reinforcement of ethical behavior. These are factors which seem to have a creative effect in various forms of psychotherapy and are also common to Ethical Therapy. In this sense, Ethical Therapy may have considerable overlap with eclectic and behavior therapies as practiced by ethical persons. However, the emphasis in Ethical Therapy is always on helping the student apply ethical principles to every facet of his life and not on any particular method.

An Ethical Therapist also does not sell his friendship but gives it freely to any ethical person and denies it to any unethical person to the best of his judgement. The selling of friendship is probably as ineffective in providing ethical growth as the sale of sex is in providing emotional growth, i.e., in satisfying our need for love. For this reason Ethical Therapists seem to be most effective when they are not professional psychotherapists, but rather, objectively creative persons who earn their living through other means and use their nonremunerative time in more formalized Ethical Therapy. However, this does not preclude professional psychotherapists also serving as Ethical Therapists.

Seeing Ethical Therapy both in its unique aspects and in its relationships to other systems which purport to provide inner peace or increase creativity, we are left with the same uncertainties which any form of therapy, physical or psychical, should arouse in us: How can we know that it works?

8

Evaluation And Practice Of Ethical Therapy

There is no guarantee that Ethical Therapy will work for anyone. If the ethical theory of chapter 6 is correct, then Ethical Therapy will definitely not work for unethical or highly neurotic persons, to say nothing of psychotics. The main purpose of Ethical Therapy is not to remove neuroses, but to prevent them. It is a type of inoculation which will protect healthy persons, but it will not necessarily cure neurotics. If the theory is correct, then healthy persons can remove their residual neuroses through Ethical Therapy. That is to say, persons who already value truth above happiness can be made free of all neuroses by crossing the threshold of morality. That this is the case is evidenced by (1) the historical example of great moral leaders, and (2) the subjective clinical evidence of the few who have tried Ethical Therapy and found that it seemed to work for them. However, this is not scientific proof.

In science, as in Ethical Therapy, one is never certain about the validity of any model of cause-and-effect relationships.

As evidence favoring a model accumulates, one becomes more confident that the model may be true, but one can neither logically nor ethically ever lose all doubts. Once doubts are lost, truth dies.

Insofar as models fail to be validated by controlled experiments, we should become ever more dubious about the truth of the model. Because it is much easier to construct apparently logical, coherent models which are false than to construct models which are true, we should assume that *all models are probably false until proven true.* Since no model is ever proven completely true, the ethical and scientific attitude to take is that the evidence supporting a model is merely indicative of some correspondence between the model and reality. Eventually all models can be shown to be inadequate for coping with some aspect of reality, viz., Newtonian Mechanics. For this reason, all models of nature must continuously evolve if truth is to grow. So it must be with Ethical Therapy.

Those who have experienced Ethical Therapy may place a high subjective probability on its validity. Those who have not experienced it should approach it in a spirit of skepticism, not faith. The only way to determine if Ethical Therapy is objectively true is by controlled experimentation.

EXPERIMENTATION

Without controlled experimentation to support it, there is no guarantee that Ethical Therapy is anything more than another form of psychofraud. This is the case no matter how strong our subjective belief about its validity may be. All forms of psychofraud have an abundance of true believers.

Since Ethical Therapy claims to work only for ethical persons, experiments to test its efficacy should be centered on ethical persons. The best objective measures for a person's ethics are the following:

1. Breadth and depth of knowledge for a given degree of intelligence and educational opportunity*
2. Index of creativity*
3. Index of destructiveness*

Breadth and Depth of Knowledge

From the definition of ethics, it follows that an ethical person will seek to continuously expand his knowledge. Because knowledge is indivisible and the universe is an interconnected whole, it follows that an ethical person will be more likely to learn many different subjects and not likely to concentrate exclusively on a single subject. The depth of knowledge will depend on the person's intelligence. The breadth of knowledge will depend on his ethics. This gives us our first criteria for selecting experimental and control groups within a democratic society having extensive educational opportunity.

1. Persons who are both highly specialized and highly intelligent are likely to be unethical and as a consequence, neurotic.
2. Highly generalized persons with some depth of knowledge in at least two important, but distinct, subjects are likely to be ethical, irrespective of their intelligence. However, the lower their intelligence for a given amount of knowledge, the more ethical they are likely to be.
3. Intelligent but ignorant persons who have had educational opportunities but failed to use them are likely to be unethical.
4. Persons who are both ignorant and of low intelligence may or may not be ethical.

* Recall Equation 1 on page 124 which gives the relationship between intelligence, ethics, creativity and destructiveness. Creativity begins with self-education.

5. Persons who are highly generalized but have no depth in any area are probably ethical if they are of low intelligence, and probably unethical if they are of high intelligence.

We have no truly good measure of intelligence. However, for the purposes of the experiment which will be proposed, it suffices to use an I.Q. type measure plus measures of imagination and force of will (50). The rationales behind I.Q.'s and their uses are given elsewhere (2, 39, 69). Tests of imagination and will are described in Guilford's *Human Intelligence* (57) and Anastasi's *Psychological Tests* (2). For our purposes we will classify persons with I.Q.'s below 90 (S.D. 15)* as *probably* having low intelligence, persons with I.Q.'s above 130 (S.D. 15) as *probably* having high intelligence, and persons in between as probably having normal intelligence. Finer classification is not meaningful with as crude an instrument as an I.Q. test. Clearly this classification is prone to some error. In general, we will classify persons in the lower 30 percent as "low," persons in the upper 2 percent as "high," and persons in between as "normal."

Given the above crude classification, we divide our experimental and control groups into normal, high and low intelligence persons. We further divide our groups into (1) generalized, (2) specialized, and (3) ignorant persons. For this purpose we can use such tests as the Graduate Record Examination for depth of knowledge in specific subjects and the Iowa Tests of Basic Skills and the U.S. Army classification tests for breadth of knowledge. The previously mentioned criteria of "low," "high" and "normal" are applied to all scores. We now divide our subjects into the following categories:

* S.D. = standard deviation. A normally distributed population is concentrated (68 percent) between plus and minus one standard deviation about the mean.

I	High Intelligence Highly Generalized Depth in at least two distinct areas	II	Normal Intelligence Highly Generalized Depth in at least one area
III	Low Intelligence Generalized Some Depth in at least one area	IV	High and Normal Intelligence Highly Specialized Some Depth only in one area
V	High and Normal Intelligence Ignorant No Depth in any area	VI	All other persons

In making the above classifications, we control for a normal range of educational opportunity, i.e., access to free or nearly free education through the college level. If someone else—our parents, the state, etc.—pays for our education, it is considered "free." This applies to most persons throughout the U.S. and Western Europe. Persons in categories I, II and III are probably ethical. Persons in categories IV and V are probably unethical. Persons in category VI are in an unknown ethical condition and will not be used in the experiment. We are now ready to further classify by creativity and destructiveness.

Creativity and Destructiveness

Creativity and destructiveness are not mutually exclusive characteristics, although they may exist on a single continuum. Some persons are both creative and destructive, e.g., Napoleon, Richard Wagner, Lenin, and Edward Teller. Others are mainly creative, e.g., J. S. Bach, Thomas Jefferson, and Albert Einstein. Still others are almost entirely destructive, e.g., Genghis Khan, Torquemada, Al Capone, and Adolf Hitler. We measure a person's creativity objectively by how much objective truth that person has engendered, i.e., by his net effect in increasing mankind's collective ability to predict and control the total environment. This is a fairly straightforward operation when the person is a scientist or technologist,* but it is very difficult to apply to contemporary artists.

The best objective criteria for the quality of art is its durability. The more persons continue to consider a particular work of art "great" over the longest period of time, the greater the art. For contemporary art we must use more subjective criteria. Probably the best criteria for the quality of contemporary art is the amount of praise it receives from persons who are objectively ethical and creative, i.e., outstanding scientists and technologists. This category would almost never include professional critics who have typically been quite blind to what is truly great in art. For example, Grieg was a highly acclaimed composer in the nineteenth century while Beethoven was lambasted during his lifetime for his best work. The same phenomena seems to occur in all the arts—painting, e.g., Rembrandt; literature, e.g., Melville; sculpture, e.g., Rodin; architecture, e.g., Wright, etc. Therefore, if artistic creativity is to be used as a criterion for total creativity, we should rate it on a subjective scale of one to ten by a panel of objectively ethical and creative scientists and technologists. Two heterogeneous panels of given degrees of objective creativity would probably be quite consistent in their artistic rating; e.g., J. S. Bach seems to be the universal favorite composer among outstanding mathematicians and theoretical scientists (182).

The objective ratings of creativity and destructiveness will have three components: (1) the amount of objective truth communicated; (2) the importance of inventions and discoveries; and (3) the importance and number of machines

* "Technologists" include teachers, engineers, physicians, craftsmen, statesmen (not politicians), etc.

constructed and maintained. In the latter case, the concept of "machine" is quite broad and includes such diverse things as houses, medicines, organizations, computers, languages, weapons, etc.

Educational, economic and engineering criteria may be applied to measure the degree of creativity: (1) the number of students taught and their scores on standardized achievement tests as previously discussed; (2) both the costs of a new invention relative to old ways of doing the same things and the number of new events which can be predicted or controlled by the new invention or scientific theory, (3) the economic return on the building or repair of machines such as vehicles or human bodies, and the amount of knowledge increased per unit cost by the machine as in (1).

The destructiveness measures would be the exact opposites of creativity measures and would include (1) the number of persons misinformed with false information (e.g., the spreading of psychofraud is destructive, since it decreases the ability to predict and control), (2) the number of persons damaged and the degree of this damage (e.g., the number of ethical persons killed or the percent of disability), and (3) the value of the property destroyed.

There are, of course, some outstanding examples of highly destructive persons such as Adolf Hitler. Most persons are not actively destructive in this way. The most common form of human destructiveness is the spreading of psychofraud or deliberate lies. In any case, with some difficulty, an objective index of creativity and destructiveness can be obtained for every person. This index can then be used further to divide our experimental and control groups. By subtracting the destructiveness index from the creativity index, we will have an index of net creativity. The upper 2 percent will be considered creative. The lower 30 percent will be considered uncreative, and the middle 68 percent, normal.

Experimental Design

If the ethical theory is correct, there should be a high positive correlation between creativity and ethics. The ethical groups should be much more creative than the unethical groups. The highly intelligent but ignorant group should be the most destructive (see Eq. 1, p. 124).

As the acid test, we divide each of the five groups randomly into several groups of equal size which should be statistically comparable. To one of the groups we apply Ethical Therapy; to the others we apply various placebos, i.e., the full spectrum of psychofraud (religion, classical psychotherapy, humanistic psychology, behaviorism, etc.). At the end of five years, we should begin to see significant differences, although some differences would begin to show immediately. The unethical groups should show no differences in creativity between those treated by Ethical Therapy and those treated by the placebo. Among the ethical groups we should expect to see a significant increase in creativity and knowledge among the group treated by Ethical Therapy over the placebo group. Clearly none of the therapists should know to which group his clients belonged nor should the evaluators of health and creativity—a triple blind placebo control.

Subjectively, the ethical groups treated by Ethical Therapy should report a decrease in anxiety and all emotions in general. Persons associated with this group should find them calmer, kinder and more pleasant to be with.

The ethical groups should, by and large, continue to get healthier than the unethical groups, independently of the therapy, until highly degenerative aging sets in. Conventional psychotherapists who are themselves objectively ethical and healthy should be shown to have a better effect on the ethical groups than their less ethical colleagues. Among the unethical groups there should be no differences as a function of treatment. The unethical groups should show a continuous degeneration of health as a function of age.

This is, of course, only a broad outline of how an experiment to test the validity of Ethical Therapy should be structured. The technical details are beyond the scope of this book. However, if Ethical Therapy is valid, the predictions made above can be verified objectively. Subjectively, any person can verify Ethical Therapy for himself.

Subjective verification will give us subjective, not objective, truth. Therefore, this should be seen as only a first step in the process of objectively verifying the validity of Ethical Therapy. Under no circumstances should a person be satisfied with subjective truth. Rather we should all use our feelings of subjective truth as a stimulus to obtaining objective verification for our hypotheses and theories. However strong our subjective beliefs, we should never cease to doubt them.

AUTO-ETHICAL THERAPY

We can all administer Ethical Therapy to ourselves by (1) consciously trying to make all decisions in our daily life on the basis of what will maximize objective truth, (2) seeking the company of persons who are or seem to be objectively ethical, i.e., persons in groups I, II, and III, and (3) avoiding persons who are or seem to be objectively unethical, i.e., persons in groups IV and V. The most difficult aspect of auto-Ethical Therapy is in consciously trying to make all decisions on the basis of what maximizes objective truth. Theoretically, all we have to do is apply the eight ethical principles of the previous chapter. This is not always easy to do. It is for this reason that the guidance of an experienced Ethical Therapist is valuable.

An Ethical Therapist is any person who deliberately follows the prime ethic and practices the eight ethical principles. Such a person may be officially designated a "psychotherapist," but more often he will be engaged in objectively creative activity and will not consider himself a psychotherapist. The vast majority of psychotherapists, as we have seen, seem to practice only psychofraud. We undergo Ethical Therapy by associating with an objectively ethical person, working with him or her and learning from him or her. We eliminate neuroses not by seeking psychotherapy but by seeking objective truth.

The most obvious first step to take in auto-Ethical Therapy is simply to educate ourselves as best we can in science, technology and the humanities. Since we are trying to maximize truth, this means we should avoid specialization and try to obtain maximum knowledge and practical experience, breadth and depth, in all the physical, biological and psychosocial sciences and their application, in order to see ourselves and the universe in an integrated evolutionary perspective. As a minimum, a person should strive to have a thorough foundation in mathematics, physical science, biology, music, literature, art, philosophy, and what few objective facts are known in the psychosocial sciences, such as history, anthropology, psychology, economics, etc. One should first obtain the rigorous foundations and then add layers of depth on a broad front.

A more detailed description of an ethical education is given elsewhere (50, 51). Here we will illustrate the application of the criterion of maximizing objective truth to the more personal decisions which must be made. It is by consciously and deliberately making our everyday decisions on the basis of ethical principles that ethics are best self-engendered. Auto-Ethical Therapy can be illustrated by a few examples.

Example 1

A person, *P*, is employed by an organization which specializes in doing contract research and development for government agencies and foundations. He is highly regarded by his colleagues and makes a lucrative and secure living with the potential for becoming independently wealthy. *P* sees that most of his work and that of his organization, although remunerative, is in no way helping any person outside of himself, his organization and the bureaucrats, who are his clients, to be happy. Although he has invented many useful devices and technologies which are highly praised by all his associates, he sees that these inventions are "shelved" by the bureaucrats and that the public, who is supposed to benefit from these developments, receives nothing. The bureaucrats take credit for his work as a means of further entrenching themselves and continue to do nothing creative. The intellectual energy and creative output of his organization, although well remunerated, is in fact being completely wasted, since (1) no one's ability to predict and control is being increased except his own, and (2) incompetent, mendacious, destructive bureaucrats are being entrenched. The choices he has are (1) to continue as he is or (2) to start a company of his own where he can develop worthwhile products which will be sold directly to the public and to industry.

The first choice will bring him the opportunity to (1) be secure, (2) become independently wealthy and (3) do intellectually stimulating work, but it (4) will not maximize objective truth. The second choice involves (1) great risk to his wealth and security and (2) the opportunity to maximize objective truth. Ethically he should take the second choice. If he does not, he will probably become neurotic. If he does, he may lose his money and his security, but he will become healthier and get closer to the threshold of morality. He will have done his best to maximize objective truth.

Example 2

P is now in business for himself and he has made a great success of it economically and ethically. He is developing many worthwhile products which are selling well and enriching him. His work is clearly expanding objective truth. However, he sees his country dominated by ignorant, unethical politicians who are waging highly destructive wars and deceiving the public for no other reason than to personally stay in power. They are doing their utmost to stifle dissent and censor the press. Their policies are such that the educational resources of the nation are withering from lack of financial support and positive direction. The youth of the country is turning more and more to drugs, hedonism and destructive ideology. Something must be done.

The choice before *P* is to risk his highly ethical and profitable business by becoming politically active or to continue as he is, expanding objective truth, enriching himself and providing security for his family. If he becomes politically active, he may be (1) harassed by the political leaders, (2) abandoned by his business associates, and (3) still probably completely unsuccessful in changing the political system. If he continues as he is, (1) the nation will probably continue to decay, but (2) he will continue to have an interesting, worthwhile and secure life.

The ethical choice is to risk everything in order to bring about ethical political change. Inaction is always unethical, and it is unethical to tolerate unethical behavior. If he does nothing, the unethical politicians will continue to destroy his and other countries until all truth is destroyed. The truth which he can engender by purely technical means can in no way compensate for the truth which is being destroyed through political means. By doing his best to improve the political system, he will also be doing his best to maximize objective truth, even if it costs him his business, his friends, and his very life. He is practicing auto-Ethical Therapy.

Example 3

Person *A* has to make the simple decision of what to do on Friday night. *A* has three choices: (1) go to a purely social function with *B*, who is sexually attractive, intellectually stimulating and a potential mate, and will go nowhere else but to the function, (2) go to a not-to-be-repeated lecture by a world renowned scientist on a very important and interesting subject; or (3) uniquely help the sole ethical political candidate, *P*, with his campaign for an important political office under circumstances given in example 2.

The ethical choice is the third one. The first choice might provide stimulating company and lead to an ethical mate, but the occasion itself is trivial. If the potential mate is truly ethical, there should be no problem. The second choice would be intellectually stimulating and increase objective truth for *A*, but it is possible to learn most of what transpired at the lecture secondhand. The third choice is the most ethical choice, because ethical political change in a society on the verge of decay is much more important than any personal experience. By helping *P* there is some chance, however small, that all of humanity may greatly benefit. If *P* and others like him are not elected, it is almost certain that objective truth will continue to be destroyed, perhaps in an irreversible process. Person *A* would maximize immediate personal truth by choice 2. Person *A* might maximize intermediate personal truth for both *A* and *B* by choice 1. However, only choice 3 has the potential for increasing truth significantly for all humanity in the long run. Therefore, in accepting choice 3, *A* is maximizing objective truth.

Example 4

Person *C* is driving legally in a strange city. A policeman stops *C* and gives him a completely unjustified traffic ticket. The policeman offers to "pay" the ticket for *C*, since *C* is from out-of-state. *C* knows immediately that the policeman is merely soliciting a bribe. Furthermore, he knows that the administration of this city is highly corrupt. The choice for *C* is to (1) pay a ten dollar bribe, or (2) spend several hundred and perhaps thousands of dollars of his time and money with little chance of success suing the policeman and the city for false charges. The ethical choice is the second one. It is unethical to tolerate unethical behavior. The policeman is clearly being unethical. Unethical means cannot produce ethical ends. Bribing the policeman is clearly unethical. Truth will be maximized if *C* spends his time and money trying to obtain justice, even if it means appealing his case to the Supreme Court.

Example 5

Person *D* lives in a police state. No criticism of the political leaders or the system is tolerated. Dissidents are often certified insane, put in asylums and have their minds destroyed with drugs and psychological torture. The choices before *D* are to (1) openly criticize the system and try, with very little probability of success, to bring about political reforms; (2) try to escape from the police state into a neighboring democratic country at the high risk of being killed or, worse still, captured; (3) go along passively with the system, not actively opposing it or supporting it; or (4) join a very small and largely ineffective underground which practices systematic terror and which has almost no chance of changing the system.

The most ethical choice is the second, because one cannot live in a police state without in some way supporting it, and it is unethical to associate with unethical persons. Furthermore, escaping from the police state is the most effective form of protest against it and only in a democratic state will *D* be free to expand truth as best he can. Also, he can best fight against the police state from abroad.

If *D* takes the first choice, he will almost certainly be destroyed, and everything he said will be distorted or suppressed by the state-controlled media. If *D* takes the third choice, he is passively acquiescing to evil by doing nothing against it; he is deliberately associating with unethical persons. If he takes the fourth choice, he will be forced to hurt innocent persons in attacking the leaders with almost no chance of bringing about reforms. One can best fight evil in association with ethical persons in democratic states. The second choice will maximize objective truth. It is auto-Ethical Therapy.

Example 6

Person *C* has been helping ethical political candidate *P* of examples 2 and 3 to the limit of his ability. He has become exhausted to the detriment of his health. *P* asks *C* to go to a critical meeting with some important supporters. If this meeting is not handled well, *P* may lose the election. No one else can handle the meeting as well as *C*, although there are other persons who could go. The choices for *C* are (1) to attend the meeting for *P* at the risk of almost certainly permanently damaging his health or (2) take some much-needed rest which has been ordered by his doctor.

Under these circumstances the ethical choice for *C* is to rest and let someone else go to the meeting. To deliberately damage one's health for any reason is unethical, because to destroy health is to destroy truth, and unethical means cannot bring about ethical ends. However, torture and martyrdom should be born if the alternative is cooperation with evil persons. It is ethical to take reasonable risks with one's health and life for an ethical cause. Great discomfort should be born for the sake of truth. However, it is unethical to decrease truth for any person, including one's self, for the alleged sake of greater truth for the majority. One need not maximize truth for one's self so long as total truth is being maximized, but truth must never be decreased for anyone, including one's self, even at the cost of one's life.

For this reason, it is unethical to smoke or take drugs, e.g., alcohol, marijuana, LSD, and heroin, which may harm the body and probably do nothing to expand objective truth (177). Abortion and suicide are also unethical for the same reasons. But private unethical acts cannot be ethically interfered with. Therefore, in an Ethical State* persons should be allowed to take any drug they wish and commit abortions and suicide. It is unethical to interfere with a person's freedom for the alleged sake of his "welfare" (50). This is why involuntary commitment of persons to psychiatric institutions is wrong. Persons who appear insane should be left alone as long as they hurt no one other than themselves. If they hurt others, they should be treated as criminals unless they voluntarily choose to be treated as mental patients.

In reality the choices are rarely as clear-cut as they were in the hypothetical examples. Most choices that have to be made are over less important matters and are not subject to purely logical analysis. They involve the use of subjective factors and evaluations. The important thing is that the person consciously considers the outcomes of his actions on the totality of objective truth before he makes a choice. If he does what he subjectively believes will maximize objective truth, he will, through a process of trial and error, eventually prove his subjective judgements objectively true.

The eight ethical principles can be applied to every aspect of our daily lives. The deliberate, purposeful following of the principles, even when logical mistakes are made, will cause any person to become increasingly ethical and less neurotic. However, only a person who is already ethical will elect to behave in this manner. Once he does, he will note an immediate improvement in his sense of psychological well-being and in his ability to interact creatively with other persons.

It is essential that persons wishing to practice Ethical

* An Ethical State is a country in which all laws and policies are formulated in accordance with the prime ethic and all logically and scientifically derived ethical principles (50).

Therapy disassociate themselves from unethical persons, who by their words or deeds communicate that they value happiness above truth. This may involve seeking new employment, friends, or even leaving one's family. But it must be done. Ethics can only flourish among ethical persons. And only persons who are developing ethically can eliminate all neuroses and destructive emotions.

SELF-EVALUATION

However Ethical Therapy has been administered, we can each evaluate its effects on ourselves. Subjectively, we can examine our own emotional state and see if we are calmer and less prone to anxiety and destructive emotions than we were in the past. Objectively, we can see if we *in fact* better predict and control our total environment. Ethical Therapy will fill us with inner peace, but so can psychofraud. It is only in the elimination of all destructive emotion, while increasing our objectively verifiable ability to predict and control our total environment, that Ethical Therapy is differentiated from psychofraud. In performing our self-evaluation of Ethical Therapy, we should go through the following steps.

1. Take a daily inventory of our emotional states and note how often we feel anxiety, fear, anger, hatred, envy, greed, jealousy, etc. If Ethical Therapy is working, we should feel less and less the power of these emotions.
2. Note how other persons react to us. If others regard us as emotional, we may still be more emotional than we thought. If we attract ever more ethical persons and gain their friendship, then Ethical Therapy is probably working.
3. Keep a written record of our predictions of physical, biological and psychosocial events. For example, if we are increasing our ability to predict (1) psychosocial events, then we should be able to correctly foresee political and social developments as well as personal behavior; (2) biological events, then we should correctly foresee the future

states of our health, the health of those around us, the ecology of the planet, etc.; and (3) physical events, then we should correctly foresee weather, astronomical happenings, the truth or falsehood of mathematical theorems, the conditions of our machines, and results of scientific experiments in physics, chemistry, geology, etc.

4. Keep a written record of our attempts to control the physical, biological and psychosocial environment. If our deliberate actions lead to predicted results in the environment, then we are controlling. If our ability to produce the results we desire is increasing, then we are increasing our ability to control. If political and social events through our actions are becoming as we wish, and we and those around us are becoming increasingly ethical, then we are better controlling our psychosocial environment. If through our actions our health and the health of those around us and the ecology of our surroundings is improving, then we are better controlling our biological environment. If our machines and our physical surroundings are, through our actions, becoming ever closer to our wishes, then we are ever better controlling our physical environment.

5. Keep an inventory of all our creative activity. If our ability to predict and control is increasing through our actions, then we are being personally creative in our own lives. If the ability of other ethical persons to predict and control is increasing through our actions, then we are being socially creative.

Although the five steps above will give us some objective criteria on our ethical progress, they are still, in part, a subjective experience, because our experiments are not well controlled. Ultimately we must subject all evaluation to objective, independently verifiable experimentation. If we cannot get anyone else to agree with our observations, we should seriously doubt the validity of our observations. It is always possible that we are right and everyone else is wrong, but it is not likely. By and large, we should value most the opinions of those who seem objectively most ethical and intelligent. We should value least, but not ignore, the opinions of those who seem objectively least ethical and intelligent. In making these judgments, ethics should be weighed more heavily than intelligence. In dealing with others, we should always listen and give them the benefit of the doubt insofar as ethics are concerned. Only unethical persons will refuse to give us honest opinions, if we ourselves are ethical.

OVERVIEW

The major impediments to Ethical Therapy and mental health are our preprogrammed, emotional patterns of behavior which drive us to seek happiness without purpose and security without truth. In reprogramming our nervous system to value truth and only truth, we are lifting ourselves by our mental bootstraps completely out of the animal plane of existence toward the ultrahuman. This is the step beyond man across the threshold of morality. It is a step which can easily make us stumble.

Virtually every form of psychofraud claims to make us better than we are. Yet we see, objectively, that for thousands of years man's progress has been limited primarily to the physical and the biological environment. There is no evidence that we, as a species, have progressed ethically. We have increased our creativity primarily through an increase in our social intelligence, i.e., the accumulation of knowledge and the evolution of our machines (50). There has been little evolutionary progress toward a systematic incorporation of ethical principles into human society. Among others, Judaism, Confucianism, Zoroastrianism, Buddhism, Christianity, Islam, and more recently democratic socialism, have made stumbling steps in the right direction. Each one of these ideologies had progressive elements which succumbed to institutionalized psychofraud. If we are to avoid self-delusion, we must subject all our models of nature, including those of personal behavior, to scientific evaluation. The Ethical State (50) is a means for us systematically and objectively to incorporate ethical principles into our sociopolitical system and scientifically evaluate their effects. Ethical Therapy is a way for us to incorporate objective ethical principles into our personal lives and evaluate their effects.

By seeing ourselves in an ethical, evolutionary perspective and doing our best to maximize objective truth, we will become increasingly ethical and help others become ethical. An increase in ethics decreases neuroses and increases creativity. Ethical Therapy will bring about this state of affairs. Ethical Therapy is both social and personal.

Social Ethical Therapy is concerned with increasing the ethics of others. Personal Ethical Therapy is concerned with increasing our own ethics. The nature of the world is such that we cannot for long increase our own ethics without increasing the ethics of others. The act of trying to increase other persons' ethics will also increase our own ethics. Social and personal Ethical Therapy are inextricably intertwined. We cannot practice one without the other, although we can emphasize one over the other. It is best to begin by emphasizing personal Ethical Therapy before attempting social Ethical Therapy.

This book has been a simple introduction to personal Ethical Therapy. *The Moral Society* (50) is a more complex, but still general, introduction to social Ethical Therapy and the broader implications of evolution and ethics. Social Ethical Therapy cannot be applied to society as a whole unless personal Ethical Therapy is first applied to the most creative persons in our society.

If the most creative persons in our society are not willing to sacrifice the maximum increase in personal truth for the sake of maximizing social truth for their children or fellowmen, then our collective neuroses will continue to increase and truth will eventually be destroyed for all mankind. Truth will be destroyed by the spontaneous and institutionalized spread of psychofraud. Currently the political system of every nation is structured to proliferate those institutions which destroy truth. These institutions are commonly called "bureaucracies."

Bureaucracies are organizations which have as their *de facto*, not *de jure*, objective the maximization of the security and happiness of their members. In so doing, they spread psychofraud and sow the seeds of their own destruction by destroying all forms of corrective criticism, because no organization, no nation, no species can long survive in the absence of objective truth. To see that this is the case, it is necessary to be ethical. To remain ethical, it is necessary to undergo and practice Ethical Therapy. Once personal Ethical Therapy has begun, social Ethical Therapy will follow.

PROJECTION

Personal Ethical Therapy will bring individual health, creativity and self-fulfillment. Social Ethical Therapy is essential to the continued evolution of our species.

The only common denominator in the entire evolutionary process is the growth in the collective intelligence of the biomass, i.e., a growth in the joint ability of all living creatures to predict and control the total environment. Intelligence can not continue to grow unless it becomes ethical, as has happened with the human species. We note that our prehuman ancestors were not unethical but merely trivial. Only a person who has been ethical can become unethical and destroy truth. Only ethics can create truth. This is the case because there is a limit to the quantity of information which can be transmitted by the genes (51, 96). Eventually, if an evolutionary nucleus is not to stagnate as did thousands of now extinct species, it must be creative. The human race has been creative for millions of years. In so doing, it has increased its collective intelligence through the accumulation of extragenetic information in the form of knowledge and machines. Simultaneously, it has grown in creativity through biological and, during the last 50,000 years, almost entirely through cultural evolution.

The only objective criterion for the ethics of a group is its creativity. The only objective criterion for the efficacy of Ethical Therapy is an increase in creativity. The human race is at a crossroads where it can (1) sink into the happy oblivion of psychofraud and become extinct or (2) *deliberately and consciously* continue its evolution through Ethical Therapy.

Almost every human being is born with the potential to become fully ethical and moral, as is evidenced by the ethics of children. Since all children increase their creativity, all persons are ethical as children. The fact that so few adults remain ethical is the result of ideology in general, institutionalized psychofraud in particular, and the immoral nature of our bureaucraticized society. These problems can all be solved practically, effectively and soon, if there is a will to solve them (50). Ethical Therapy is essential to their solution.

Without Ethical Therapy in some form, i.e., without positive reinforcement of inborn, naturally ethical behavior, all persons become unethical and destructive. With Ethical Therapy almost all persons can become ethical and creative, if they have not already become unethical. Each ethical person can become a nucleus of expanding ethical intelligence for himself and others. By simply being himself, an ethical person is both a practitioner and a recipient of Ethical Therapy.

Ethical Therapy is based not on a specific method, but on a general goal. It is based on the goal of expanding ethical intelligence as best we can for ourselves and others. This is an infinite goal which will never be reached by us or our progeny, but it is a goal to which we, as a species, can always move ever closer as we grow in ethics, intelligence and creativity. It is the only goal whose pursuit can bring us unending joy as a trivial consequence of our conscious evolution toward infinite ethical intelligence.

To create a group, a nation and a world dedicated to the unending expansion of ethical intelligence is the means and the end of Ethical Therapy. Those who practice Ethical Therapy will undergo it. Those who undergo Ethical Therapy are practicing it. All who are or shall become a part of Ethical Therapy are also a part of the infinitely evolving ethical intelligence of the universe. The means are the ends. This is the Cosmic Moral Society. This is unending evolution. It is something worth striving for.

Glossary

ABERRANT Descriptive term applied to actions or things which deviate from what is considered normal and proper by the person(s) applying the term.

ART A process for increasing truth by a symbolic communication of complex patterns directly to the unconscious mind.

ASYMPTOTIC A process by which something gets ever closer to something else but never reaches it.

BEHAVIOR Divided into subjective and objective behavior. Subjective behavior refers to actions observable only by the person behaving, e.g., thinking. Objective behavior refers to actions observable by more than one person, e.g., speaking.

BEHAVIORISM A system of psychology and psychotherapy which states that all models of behavior must be based *entirely* on measurable objective behavior. This system denies the existence of subjective behavior. Behaviorism has been effective in predicting and controlling simple animal and human behavior. It has not been shown to increase creativity significantly.

BIOMASS The totality of all living creatures which inhabit the earth at any given instant. Sometimes called the *instantaneous biosphere.*

BUREAUCRACY An organization which destroys truth by seeking to destroy all means of detecting its errors and shortcomings. A bureaucracy operates without utilizing feedback and self correction. Whatever its *de jure* purposes, a bureaucracy's *de facto* purpose is limited to enhancing the security of its members.

CERTAINTY A state of mind in which no doubt exists about some cause-and-effect relationships. It is unethical to be certain about anything except the existence of our own thoughts and perceptions, which are not cause-and-effect relationships. The need for certainty may be the fatal blow in human nature. Through Ethical Therapy, humanity can learn to cope with the insecurity of uncertainty. One cannot learn when one is certain.

CONSCIOUS Refers to that state of mind in which we can predict and control our own throughts and perceptions. The conscious mind is the set of all our predictable and controllable thoughts and perceptions.

CONTROL The deliberate causal formation of a predicted set of events. The only common denominator in evolution is an increasing ability to predict and control the total environment. To control an event is to cause it to behave as we wish. The event can include our own thoughts or any external action in the physical, biological or psychosocial environment.

CREATIVITY The ability to organize the total environment—physical, biological and psychosocial—into new patterns which increase the collective ability of all ethical persons to predict and control their total environment, while not decreasing this ability for any ethical person. Creativity is a direct function of intelligence and ethics.

$C \simeq I E$

Where: C = Creativity in quanta of knowledge generated per unit time. Range $(-\infty,\infty)$.

I = Intelligence in quanta of knowledge controlled per unit time. Range $(0, \infty)$.

E = Ethics, a dimensionless quantity between -1 and +1 representing the fraction of time spent decreasing truth (negative) or increasing truth (positive).

$\simeq$ indicates an approximation.

DESTRUCTIVENESS The disorganization of the total environment into patterns which decrease the ability of any or all ethical persons to predict and control their total environment—physical, biological and psychosocial. Negative creativity.

DISEASE Any condition of an organism acquired through heredity or environment which decreases its intelligence, i.e., ability to predict its total environment—physical, biological and psychosocial.

EDUCATION Any process which increases objective truth for any organism, i.e., any process which increases any organism's ability to predict and control by increasing or altering the information content of the organism.

EMOTION A preprogrammed pattern of behavior, which predisposes an organism to behave aggressively, fearfully, lovingly, or in some combination of these patterns. The basic emotions are inborn and instinctive but can be modified by learning.

ENTROPY A condition of chaos and disorder as well as a force which increases the chaos and disorder in the universe. Whatever decreases objective truth increases entropy and vice-versa.

ENVIRONMENT The total environment has three primary dimensions—the physical, biological and psychosocial. The physical includes all matter, natural laws and their interactions. The biological includes all living organisms. The psychosocial includes all the behavior of all living organisms.

ETHICAL Behavior is ethical if and only if it increases objective truth over all time and space. A person is ethical if the net effect of his actions is to increase objective truth. An ethical person may occasionally behave unethically.

ETHICAL INTELLIGENCE The ability to predict and control the total environment creatively.

ETHICAL STATE A social and

political system dedicated and structured to maximize the expansion of objective truth. This is the transition society between our current social and political system and the Moral Society.

ETHICAL THERAPY A process for increasing creative intelligence by increasing ethics. The immediate objective is to reorient the ethical perspective of the person so that he uses the criterion of what maximizes objective truth in making every decision and relating to other persons. This process also eliminates neuroses and emotional blockages to creative behavior. It is not effective with psychotics or with unethical persons.

ETHICS Rules of optimal behavior which simultaneously maximize our ability to achieve all logically consistent goals. It can be shown logically and scientifically that rules of behavior are optimal if and only if they satisfy the criterion of maximizing objective truth.

EVIL Any action or thing which causes a net decrease in objective truth.

EVOLUTION A process which increases the intelligence in the universe. The only common denominator in the evolutionary process is the increasing ability of the biomass to predict and control its total environment. When intelligence can predict and control itself, it has become ethical. Man is the only species known which can predict and control its own intelligence. This manifests itself in all creative behavior and cultural evolution.

GENERALIST (Scientific Generalist) A person who has a broad understanding of *all* the knowledge of his or her contemporaries. The generalist is capable of predicting and controlling all aspects of the total environment—physical, biological and psychosocial—to the same degree. (See *Specialist*) A generalist may have as much or more depth than a specialist in any area. A scientific generalist has depth in all fields of science. A person with no depth in science may be a generalist, but he is generally ignorant.

GOOD Any action or thing which causes a net increase in objective truth.

HAPPINESS A state of mind in which a person believes that his desires are *being* fulfilled. When the desires being fulfilled are stronger than the desires unfulfilled, the net effect is happiness. When the converse is the case, the net effect is unhappiness.

HEALTH The physical and mental condition conducive to predicting controlling the total environment. Whatever diminishes our ability to predict and control the total environment diminishes our health. When this occurs through physiological change, such as a broken leg, then it is our physical health that is diminished. When this occurs through a change in the information content of our mind, then it is mental health that has been diminished and we say that the person is neurotic. When there is a combination of deleterious physiological and information changes in the nervous system, the person may become psychotic. The best objective indicator of health is creativity. Unethical persons are neither healthy nor creative.

HETEROSEXUAL A type of behavior in which an organism shows a clear preference for the companionship of the opposite sex in general and seeks to mate with the opposite sex in particular. The bulk of the scientific evidence is that this type of behavior is primarily biologically determined, although it can be modified by conditioning.

HOMOSEXUAL A type of behavior in which an organism shows a

preference for the companionship of members of its own sex in general and seeks to mate with its own sex in particular. The bulk of the scientific evidence is that this type of behavior is determined primarily by biology but that it may be modified by conditioning.

HUMANISTIC PSYCHOLOGY An eclectic, ill-defined system of psychology based on the theories of Abraham Maslow. The basic assumption is that there is a hierarchy of human needs—security, love, self-esteem and self-actualization. Persons cannot progress satisfactorily to satisfying higher needs if lower needs are unsatisfied. A healthy person is self-actualizing. This school has gone far beyond Maslow and now embraces every conceivable form of psychofraud from witchcraft to sex therapy. In its most extreme forms, humanistic psychology does not distinguish between healthy and aberrant behavior. Anything which causes happiness and no unhappiness is regarded as "good."

IATROGENIC Refers to harm or illness brought about by improper medical treatment.

IDEOLOGY Any process or system of beliefs which claims to be able to predict and control some or all aspects of the total environment without showing scientifically that this is in fact the case. Ideologies are based on faith and are emotionally defended against any scientific contradiction. They include religion, witchcraft, Marxism and all forms of psychofraud in general.

IGNORANCE A lack of important correct information within the nervous system of an organism.

IMMORAL A type of behavior in which all actions either decrease objective truth, i.e., are destructive, or are trivial. A person becomes immoral if and only if he sees happiness as the only purpose of life and cares nothing for objective truth. The more intelligent an immoral person is the more destructive he will be. Immoral persons never behave ethically again once they become immoral.

IMPORTANT Refers to anything which significantly either increases or decreases objective truth.

INFORMATION The symbolic representation of events and their relationships. Information is an essential component of intelligence. An entity devoid of information is devoid of intelligence.

INTELLIGENCE The ability to predict and control the total environment—physical, biological and psychosocial. Intelligence seems to be primarily an organic phenomenon which is modified by environmental factors, specifically the information acquired. When true information is incorporated into intelligence, it is called "knowledge."

KNOWLEDGE Information which enables or increases the ability of an organism to predict and control its total environment, i.e., information which is true and increases intelligence and health. Knowledge cannot exist independently of intelligence. A book contains information. Only an intelligent organism has knowledge.

LOVE Refers to a type of behavior as well as to an emotion. As an emotion it is a preprogrammed state of mind which predisposes us to behave in such a way as to enhance the welfare of another even at the cost of our own welfare. When welfare is seen as synonymous with happiness, then love is perverse and unethical. When welfare is seen as synonymous with creative intelligence, then love is natural and ethical. Ethical love can exist without emotion, as when a person makes a deliberate rational choice to maximize objective truth as an end in itself and increases the creative intelligence of others as a necessary means toward this end. Emotional love can be ethical as in the case of protective nurturing and maternal instincts. Emotional love is easy to pervert as in the case of sadomasochists and also of parents who sacrifice objective truth for the happiness of their children.

MACHINE A manufactured device which converts one form of energy into another. Language, drugs, tools, telescopes, computers, radios, clothing, organizations and houses are all examples of machines. The increasing ability to make and use machines is the basis of human evolution. Machines are amplifiers of intelligence.

MIND The set of all our thoughts and perceptions. Insofar as thoughts and perceptions are predictable and controllable, the mind is conscious. Insofar as thoughts are unpredictable and uncontrollable, the mind is unconscious. We know with certainty only the existence of our own minds. We infer from the behavior of other organisms and our own behavior and minds that other organisms have minds similar to our own insofar as they behave similarly to us. From this inference we can develop a mind model of behavior which can be objectively shown to enable us to predict and control behavior. The mind model is analogous to the model of gravity. We cannot perceive directly the existence of gravity, but it is a model which enables us to predict and control.

MORAL A type of behavior in which all actions either increase objective truth or are trivial. A person becomes moral if and only if he sees the maximal expansion of objective truth as the only purpose of life and is indifferent to anyone's happiness, including his own. The more intelligent a moral person is, the more creative he will be. A moral person never behaves unethically again after becoming moral. Moral persons are devoid of emotions. They behave lovingly toward ethical persons, but this is not a preprogrammed pattern of behavior but a logical consequence of their desire to maximize objective truth.

MORAL SENSE The genetically determined program, apparently unique to the human species, which makes man value truth above happiness. The Moral Sense is easily perverted into self-righteousness and intolerance by unethical persons who may believe they have already found truth.

MORAL SOCIETY A social union of moral persons united by ethical love into a collective intelligence with the single purpose of maximizing the expansion of creative intelligence throughout the universe.

MYSTICISM Any systematic attempt to obtain truth through direct insight independently of scientific evidence and processes. Mystical truth is always of subjective origin. When mystical insights are supported by scientific evidence, then the mystical truth has become objective. There is no conflict between mysticism and science as long as mystical insights are not held to represent a higher reality than objective truth. It is in the nature of mysticism that its adherents tend to substitute subjective truth for objective truth and in the process become practitioners of psychofraud. All the major religions and the traditional ethical and psychotherapeutic systems seem to have a mystical basis. Objective evolutionary ethics and Ethical Therapy have a strictly scientific basis.

NEUROSES Learned patterns of behavior which decrease a person's ability to predict and control his total environment. Uncontrollable emotionalism is not necessarily neurotic unless it has been caused by some learned experience; e.g., persons who are filled with hate for some particular ethnic group are neurotic because it is necessary to learn to hate a whole ethnic group, and this behavior decreases creative intelligence. Because neurotic behavior is learned behavior, it is susceptible to modification by all types of psychofraud as well as Ethical Therapy.

"THE NEW MAGIC" A synthesis between mysticism, psychotherapy, hedonism and some scientific facts.

ORGANIZATION A group of persons united by a set of commonly held and accepted purposes and rules of behavior. When an organization is ethical, it increases objective truth for all ethical persons. When it is unethical, it becomes a bureaucracy and destroys objective truth as a means of increasing the security and happiness of its members.

PERSONALITY A subset of "intelligence" which determines what will be predicted and controlled and the resolve to accomplish its ends.

PERSONAL MORALITY (Personal Ethics) The desire to expand our own personal creative intelligence without decreasing the creative intelligence of any person.

PERVERSE Refers to any behavior which increases or seeks to increase happiness without increasing objective truth. A pervert is a person who systematically increases his own happiness without increasing anyone's creative intelligence, including his own.

PREDICT AND CONTROL Refers to the essential property of intelligent organisms by which events are foreseen and made to comply with the organism's needs and desires. The ability to predict cannot exist independently of the ability to control and vice-verse. Although man could predict astronomical events long before he could control them (as in the case of artificial satellites), he could not have predicted any astronomical events if he could not have controlled his observational procedures by controlling his own biological sensors (eyes, ears, etc.) and the creation of amplifiers of his sensors, such as clocks, calendars and telescopes. Any event which is controlled is by definition predicted. Therefore, control is a higher property of intelligence than prediction, although each property is essential to the other. See definitions of *Prediction* and of *Control.*

PREDICTION The activity of correctly imagining an event before it is objectively perceived. The ability to predict precedes the ability to control and is essential to the evolutionary process.

PROGRESS Anything which increases creative intelligence represents a progressive force. Progress is the process of expanding objective truth within the universe and is synonymous with evolution.

PSYCHOFRAUD An ideology about human behavior. Any model which purports to predict and control human behavior and cannot be scientifically verified is psychofraud. Examples of psychofraud are found in all religions, political ideologies, and forms of psychotherapy.

PSYCHOSIS Compulsive destructive behavior. An extreme form of neurosis which involves organic factors. These predispose the psychotic to acquire information which grossly distorts reality. Corrective treatment is ineffective unless the basic organic factors have also been corrected. Many forms of psychotic behavior are at least partially corrected with vitamins and drugs.

PSYCHOTHERAPY A process for replacing information which decreases a person's ability to predict and control his total environment with information which increases his ability to predict and control his total environment. Psychotherapy is a special type of education and does not necessarily include the use of drugs or surgery, although these techniques can also change behavior and possibly even increase creativity. The best criterion for the success of psychotherapy is an increase in the net creativity of the person. Most of the treatments called psychotherapy seem to consist mainly of psychofraud.

PROGRAMMING The encoding of information into a system. Human beings are totally programmed by heredity and their environment.

RATIONAL Any action or thing which is logically self-consistent and does not involve internal contradictions. In the real world things are only relatively rational, since almost every model and person has some internal contradictions, although they may not be apparent. This results mainly from a lack of scientific knowledge, not necessarily poor logic. Newton's model of the universe was more rational than that of Aristotle but less rational than that of Einstein, although all these models were highly rational in relationship to the more popular models of their day.

REALITY That which we can (1) predict and control or (2) know that we can neither predict nor control. Our thoughts and perceptions are always real but not the models we create about what causes our thoughts and preceptions. Only that which is true is real. Only models which enable us to predict and control are true.

RELIGION Any ideology which seeks to explain the basic causes and purposes of the universe and stresses means for predicting and controlling our thoughts and perceptions beyond the limits of our lives. In religion, the most important truths are assumed to be known, and new "truths" are accepted only insofar as they support the basic assumptions. Religions are created in an ethical attempt to create a coherent model of the universe and man's relationship to it. Religions become evil only because they are closed systems which do not accept information contradicting the basic ideology. It is the Moral Sense which continuously causes man to seek the one true religion. It is the immoral sense which makes him believe he has found it.

SANITY That property of mind which permits it to cope rationally with problems and to see things as they objectively exist.

SCIENCE (Scientific Method) A process for expanding objective truth. It is based on the notion that all models of cause-and-effect relationships are assumed to be probably false until proven true by controlled experiments. No model is ever assumed to be beyond doubt. It is assumed that every model of cause-and-effect relationships can always be improved.

SCIENTIFIC ILLITERATE A person who has little or no scientific knowledge, i.e., knowledge obtained through the scientific method. In general, a person who has no systematic knowledge of mathematics, physical science or biology is a scientific illiterate. In general, scientific illiterates are victims and practitioners of psychofraud. Specialized scientists tend to succumb to ideology in those parts of the environment about which they have little or no scientific knowledge. Since there is so little scientific knowledge of the psychosocial environment, this is the major area of ideology and psychofraud. All persons tend to create the illusion that they can predict and control their total environment.

Therefore, they fill their minds with psychofraud and ideology when they are not scientific generalists.

SCIENTIFIC GENERALIST (See *Generalist*)

SECURITY A state of mind in which a person believes he has or can readily obtain everything he needs and has no fear of losing what he already has. Security is an idealized state which no one ever fully reaches except by self-delusion or by becoming moral. Neuroses as well as psychoses may develop in a deluded attempt to become moral.

SICKNESS (See *Disease*)

SOCIAL MORALITY (Social Ethics) The desire to expand the creative intelligence of other persons without decreasing any person's creative intelligence including our own.

SOCIAL SCIENCE Any of the numerous attempts to develop scientific models of human behavior, e.g., economics, psychology and sociology. In fact, most social science models are psychofraud which have never been objectively shown to predict and control human behavior.

SOUL The notion of "soul" is logically equivalent to the notion of "mind," the difference being that the concept of soul is usually tied to supernatural cause-and-effect relationships which are ideologically based and represent psychofraud. The concept of mind can be completely scientific but may involve psychofraud, as in psychoanalysis.

SPECIALIST A person who has learned about one limited aspect of the total environment at the expense of remaining extremely ignorant of the rest of the environment. The specialist is distinguished from the generalist not by what he knows but by what he does not know. A generalist may have as much depth as the specialist in his own speciality.

TOTAL ENVIRONMENT Includes all that can be perceived or conceived. It includes the (1) physical—matter, energy and all their interrelationships; (2) biological—all forms of life, their structures and interrelationships; (3) psychosocial—all manifestations of mind, behavior and their interrelationships.

TRIVIAL Refers to activity or things which neither increase nor decrease objective truth. This is an idealized situation which exists mainly as an approximation of reality. In fact, it can probably be shown that almost any action will produce either a net ethical or unethical effect.

TRUTH Refers only to *working* descriptions and models of events and their relationships. A model of cause-and-effect relationships is true only insofar as it enables us to predict and control. Truth is subjective insofar as we believe that we can predict and control. Subjective truth, or intuition, is often the first step of developing objective truth but until verified may include many false insights and concepts. Psychofraud can engender subjective truth. Only science engenders objective truth.

UNCONSCIOUS Refers to those thoughts and perceptions which we can neither predict nor control. Uncontrollable emotions, post-hypnotic suggestions and forgotten events which are spontaneously remembered are examples of unconscious processes. Creative endeavor seems to involve considerable unconscious as well as conscious activity.

UNETHICAL Refers to behavior or persons which decrease objective truth and are destructive. A person is unethical if the net effect of his actions decreases creative intelligence. An unethical person may occasionally behave ethically, although this becomes infrequent with time once a person has become unethical.

Appendix

Definitions, Axioms and Theorems

1. Human beings have two and only two *basic* goals—happiness and/or truth.

2. *Objective truth* is measured entirely by how much it increases our ability to predict and control the total environment—physical, biological and psychosocial.

3. The total environment transcends all time and space.

4. *Happiness* is the *subjective belief* that our strongest desires are *being* fulfilled.

5. An *ethical person* is one in whom the basic desire for *objective* truth is stronger than the basic desire for happiness. He may occasionally behave unethically.

6. An *unethical person* is one in whom the basic desire for happiness is stronger than the basic desire for objective truth. He may occasionally behave ethically.

7. A *moral person* has *objective truth* as his *sole* desire, and he cares nothing for his or any other person's happiness. He never behaves unethically.

8. An *immoral person* has *happiness* as his *sole* desire, and he cares nothing for objective truth. He never behaves ethically.

9. To be *creative* is to organize the environment into new

patterns which increase the ability of at least one ethical person to predict and control the total environment while not decreasing any ethical person's ability.

10. To be *destructive* is to disorganize the environment into patterns which decrease at least one ethical person's ability to predict and control the total environment.

11. Destruction, however minor, can never increase creativity.

12. The more unethical a person is, the more destructive he will be for a given level of intelligence.

13. Immoral persons can only destroy; they never create again once they are immoral.

14. The more ethical a person, the more creative he will be for a given level of intelligence.

15. Moral persons will only create; they never destroy again once they become moral.

16. Ethics are relative, but morality is absolute.

17. Ethics exist on a continuum with purely creative behavior at one extreme and purely destructive behavior at the other extreme; the midpoint is the dividing line of trivia between ethical and unethical behavior.

18. The more ethical a person is, the less neurotic he will be for a given biological endowment.

19. Moral persons are devoid of all neuroses.

20. *Neuroses* are learned patterns of behavior which decrease a person's ability to predict and control his total environment.

21. The creativity of moral persons is limited only by their intelligence.

22. *Intelligence* is the ability to predict and control the total environment.

23. The communication of objective truth increases intelligence but does not necessarily increase creativity.

24. To increase the intelligence of unethical persons in general and immoral persons in particular is to increase their ability to destroy.

25. To increase the intelligence of ethical persons in general and moral persons in particular is to increase their ability to create.

26. Ethical Therapy is a means of increasing a person's desire for objective truth.

27. The successful application of Ethical Therapy will make ethical persons moral.

28. All human beings are born ethical, as is evidenced by the fact that they grow in creativity while they are children.

29. Persons become unethical by environmental factors which condition them through the applications of pain and pleasure to value happiness above objective truth.

30. Persons remain ethical and become moral because of environmental factors which condition them through pain and pleasure to value objective truth above happiness.

31. Truth is always a source of happiness, i.e., a reward, for moral persons.

32. For persons who are not moral, truth is a source of happiness, i.e., a reward, if and only if it confirms their prejudices and positive expectations; otherwise it is a punishment, i.e., a source of unhappiness.

33. Subjective truth can be as strong a reward as objective truth for persons who are not moral.

34. A moral person is rewarded only by objective truth.

35. Psychofraud is a process which uses subjective truth, and only subjective truth, as a reward; it is an unscientific psychosocial model.

36. Ethical Therapy is a process which uses objective truth, and only objective truth, as a reward.

37. The more unethical a person becomes, the less likely it is that objective truth will reward him, since happiness is increasingly his sole objective and happiness can easily be engendered by psychofraud.

38. The happiness of all immoral persons and most unethical persons is dependent on the illusions of psychofraud.

39. All unethical persons will resist any attempt to expose the psychofraud which they have embraced.

40. Persons embrace psychofraud only as a means of being happy.

41. To believe that one can predict and control any aspect of the total environment always makes persons happy.

42. To believe that one cannot predict and control some aspect of the total environment makes all persons who are not moral unhappy.

43. The part of the total environment which persons desire most to predict and control is their own mind.

44. Persons become unethical if they use psychofraud as a means

of predicting and controlling their own thoughts and perceptions.

45. Dependency on psychofraud destroys the potential for ethical development.

46. Ethical Therapy can only succeed with ethical persons; it will fail with any unethical person.

47. Unethical persons can never again be made ethical; if given the opportunity, they will decrease the ethics of those who still are ethical but not yet moral.

48. If Ethical Therapy is to succeed, ethical persons must disassociate from unethical persons.

49. Ethical Therapy is administered by association with ethical persons.

50. Ethical Therapy is best administered by moral persons.

51. Only an ethical person can be an Ethical Therapist.

52. The greater the ethics of the persons with whom we associate, the greater will be the Ethical Therapeutic effect.

53. The more ethical and the fewer unethical persons we associate with, the greater will be the Ethical Therapeutic effect.

54. An ethical person can be his own Ethical Therapist, although this is the least effective form of Ethical Therapy.

55. Auto-Ethical Therapy involves consciously using objective truth as the criterion by which all decisions are made.

56. The more often objective truth is used as a criterion for making decisions, the more ethical the person will become.

57. The more often happiness is used as a criterion for making decisions, the less ethical a person will become.

58. Although subjective truth can be a valid ethical criterion for making decisions, it is invalid (1) when it conflicts with objective truth and (2) when it is used as a *sole* criterion and never subjected to objective scientific tests.

59. The effects of Ethical Therapy, however applied, are (1) increased creativity and (2) a decrease in neuroses.

60. An increase in creativity is an objective measure of Ethical Therapeutic effectiveness.

61. A decrease in neurosis as manifested by a decrease in our own anxiety and destructive emotions is a subjective test of Ethical Therapeutic effectiveness.

62. Emotions are genetically preprogrammed patterns of behavior which predispose us to act fearfully, aggressively or lovingly—independently of any logical analysis of the ethical consequences of our acts.

63. The more ethical we become, the less our actions are determined by emotions.

64. A moral person is devoid of *all* emotions, but not of sensitivity, human warmth, joy, aesthetic sensibility or ethical love.

65. Ethical love is not an emotion, but a deliberate, logical choice made to increase the intelligence of another person for the purpose of maximizing objective truth.

66. Emotional love as well as fear and aggression can serve ethical purposes and are essential to the evolution of a species and an individual; however, these emotions are easily perverted and can become destructive in an unethical environment.

67. The more unethical a person becomes, the more that person seeks to cater to his emotional whims irrespective of their ethical effects, although an unethical person may be very logical and deliberate in satisfying his emotional needs, e.g., Hitler and Stalin.

68. Only actions which increase objective truth (i.e., ethical intelligence and creativity) are ethical.

69. Any action which decreases objective truth (i.e., ethical intelligence and creativity) for any person is unethical.

70. Unethical means can never achieve ethical ends.

71. Means which are not ends are never ethical.

72. It is unethical to tolerate unethical behavior.

73. It is unethical to be certain.

74. It is ethical to doubt.

75. Inaction is unethical.

76. Ethical Therapy is based on the application of the preceding eight ethical principles to every aspect of our lives.

77. A society which incorporates the eight ethical principles into all its decisions is an Ethical State.

78. Only ethical persons can create an Ethical State.

79. Only an Ethical State can create a Moral Society.

80. In a Moral Society all persons become moral and fully creative; it is the evolutionary destiny of the human race.

Bibliography

1. Alland, A. *Evolution of Human Behavior*. Garden City, New York: The Natural History Press, 1967.

2. Anastasi, Anne. *Psychological Testing*, 3rd ed. New York: Macmillan, 1968.

3. Ansensio, J. R. "Suicide Among Doctors." *British Medical Journal* 1: 789-790, 1964.

4. Ariens-Kappers, C. U. *The Evolution of the Nervous System*, Haarlem: De Erven F. Bohn, 1929.

5. Armor, D. J. *School Bussing and Academic Achievement*. Cambridge: Harvard University Press, May 1972.

6. Bergin, A. E. and S. W. Garfield. *Handbook of Psychotherapy and Behavior Change: An Empirical Approach*, New York: Wiley, 1971.

7. Bergin, A. E. and H. H. Strupp. *Changing Frontiers in the Science of Psychotherapy*. Chicago: Aldine-Atherton, 1972.

8. Blachly, P. H., et al. "Suicide in Professional Groups." *New England Journal of Medicine* 268: 1278-1282, 1963.

9. Bloom, Victor. "An Analysis of Suicide at a Training Center." *American Journal of Psychiatry* 123(8): 918-925, 1967.

10. Bockoven, J. S. *Moral Treatment*. New York City: Springer, 1963.

11. Bogoch, S. *Biochemistry of Memory*. New York: Oxford University Press, 1968.

12. Bonin, G. von. *The Evolution of the Human Brain*. Chicago: University of Chicago Press, 1963.

13. Borst, L. V. *Mind-Brain Identity Theory*. New York: Macmillan, 1970.

14. Breed, Warren. "Occupational Mobility and Suicide Among White Males." *American Sociology Review* 28(2): 179-180, 1963.

15. Brenner, B. "Suicide and Occupation." *American Sociology Review* 24:86, 1959.

16. Brun, J. *Socrates*. New York: Walker, 1962.

17. Castañeda, C. *The Teachings of Don Juan*. Berkeley: University of California Press, 1968.

18. Castañeda, C. *A Separate Reality*. New York: Simon and Schuster, 1971.

19. Cattell, R. D. *Crooked Personalities*. New York: D-Appleton-Century Co., 1938.

20. Chang, Carsun. *Neoconfuciust Thought*. New Haven, Conn: College and University Press, 1963.

21. Chauchard, P. *Hypnosis and Suggestion*. New York: Walker and Co., 1964.

22. Chauchard, P. *Les Sciences du Cerveau*. Paris: Dunod, 1966.

23. Chertok, L. *Hypnosis*. New York: Pergamon, 1966.

24. Chesler, Phyllis. *Women and Madness*. New York: Doubleday, 1972.

25. Chessick, R. D. *How Psychotherapy Heals*. New York: Science House, 1969.

26. Chiang, Hung-Min and A. Maslow. *The Healthy Personality*. New York: Van Nostrand Reinhold, 1969.

27. Child, C. M. et al. *The Unconscious: A Symposium*. Freeport, New York City: Books for Libraries Press, Inc., 1966.

28. Chu, Franklin, et al. *Nader Report on Mental Health in the U.S.*, announced in 1972.

29. Cohen, Victor. "A Future Society of Patients?" *Washington Post*, June 11, 1972, p. K1.

30. Creel, H. G. *Confucius and the Chinese Way*. New York: Harper Torch, 1960.

31. Das, S. S. *Hypnosis: Clinical*. New York: Asia Publishing House, 1966.

32. Deutscher, I. *The Biography of Leon Trotsky. The Prophet Armed, vol. 1; The Prophet Unarmed, vol. 2; The Prophet Outcast, vol. 3;* New York, London: Oxford Press, 1970.

33. Dollard, J. *Project M-648*. U.S. Public Health Service Report No. M-648, 1955.

34. Eccles J. C. *Brain—The Unity of Conscious Experience*. New York: Cambridge University Press, 1965.

35. Eddy, M. B., et al. (a) *Science and Health*; (b) *A Century of Christian Science Healing*. Boston: Christian Science Publishing Society, 1966.

36. Ehrenwald, J. *Psychotherapy: Myth and Method*. New York: Grune & Stratton, 1966.

37. Ehrkardt, Anke, and John Money. *Ten Young Girls Masculinized in Utero*. Baltimore: Psychonormal Research Unit, Johns Hopkins Medical School, 1967.

38. Eysenck, H. J., and S. Rachman. *The Causes and Cures of Neuroses.* San Diego: Robert R. Knapp, 1965.

39. Eysenck, H. J. *The I.Q. Argument*. New York: Library Press, 1971.

40. Farberow, N. L. *Bibliography on Suicide and Suicide Prevention*. Washington: U.S. Govt. Printing Office, 1968.

41. Fleisher, J. *Suicide—Man's Fate,* D.T.R.B. Ed. New York: 1970.

42. Frank, J. D. "Therapeutic Factors in Psychotherapy." *American Journal of Psychotherapy*, July, 1971.

43. Frank, J. D. "The Bewildering World of Psychotherapy." *Journal of Social Issues* 28:4, 1972.

44. Frazer, J. *The Golden Bough*, Revised by T. H. Gaster. New York: Mentor, 1964.

45. Frederick, C. J., Ed. *The Future of Psychotherapy*. Boston: Little, Brown and Company, 1969.

46. Freedland, N. *The Occult Explosion*. New York: G. P. Putnam's Sons, 1972.

47. Freeman, W. *The Psychiatrist*. New York: Grune and Stratton, 1967.

48. Freeman, Walter. "Psychiatrists Who Kill Themselves: A Study in Suicide." *American Journal of Psychiatry* 124(6):846-847, 1967.

49. Freud, S. *The Basic Writings.* New York: Random House, various editions.

50. Garcia, J. D. *The Moral Society: A Rational Alternative to Death*. New York: Julian Press, 1971. (Currently available through Whitmore)

51. Garcia, J. D. *The Step Beyond Man* (An elementary textbook in integrated science, deriving a general theory of evolution and its psychosocial and ethical implications). To be published by Whitmore in 1975.

52. Goldenson, R. M. *The Encyclopedia of Human Behavior*, Vol. I, II. New York: Doubleday, 1970.

53. Goldstein, K. *Human Nature*. New York City: Schocken, 1963.

54. Gregory, M. *Psychotherapy: Religious and Scientific*. New York: Macmillan, 1939.

55. Grossman, S. P. *A Textbook of Physiological Psychology*, New York: John Wiley & Sons, Inc., 1967.

56. Grossman, R. *The Structure of Mind*. Wisconsin University Press, 1965.

57. Guilford, J. *The Nature of Human Intelligence*. New York: McGraw-Hill, 1967.

58. Hadfield, B. A. *Introduction to Psychotherapy*. Bristol: J. W. Arrowsmith Ltd., 1967.

59. Hilgard, E. R. *Experience of Hypnosis*. New York: Harcourt, Brace and World, 1968.

60. Hoyle, F. *Galaxies, Nuclei and Quasars*. New York: Harper & Row, 1965.

61. Hoyle, F. *From Stonehenge To Modern Cosmology*. Cambridge: Cambridge University Press, 1972.

62. Hull, C. L. *Hypnosis and Suggestability*. New York: Appleton-Century-Crofts, 1968.

63. Hyden, H., et al. *On the Biology of Learning*. New York: Harcourt, Brace and World, 1969.

64. Isaacs, M. L. *Personality Dimensions Associated with Positive Placebo Reaction*. Washington: Catholic University of America Press, 1959.

65. Janov, A. *The Primal Scream*. New York: Delta, 1970.

66. Janov, A. *The Anatomy of Mental Illness*. New York: G. P. Putnam's Sons, 1972.

67. Jefferson, T. *On Democracy*, various editions. See, e.g., S. K. Padover, *The Complete Jefferson*. Duell Press, 1943, and other studies by Padover.

68. Jencks, C., et al. *Inequality: A Reassessment of the Effect of Family and Schooling in America.* New York: Basic Books, Inc., 1972.

69. Jensen, A. "Environment, Heredity and Intelligence." Reprint Series, No. 2, *Harvard Educational Review,* 1969. Also see *Educability and Group Differences.* New York: Harper & Row, 1973.

70. Jung, C. G. *The Collected Works.* London: Rutledge and K. Paul, 1966.

71. Kadushin, C. *Why People Go to Psychotherapists.* New York: Atherton Press, 1969.

72. Karamyan, A. I. *Evolution of the Cerebellum and Cerebal Hemispheres.* National Science Foundation, 1962.

73. Kissel, P. and D. Barraucand. *Placebos et Effet Placebo En Médecine.* Paris: Masson, et Cie., 1964.

74. Koch, Sigmund. "Can Psychology Be A Coherent Science?" *Psychology Today, July, 1971,* p. 14.

75. Konorski, J. *Integrative Activity of the Brain.* Chicago: University of Chicago Press, 1967.

76. Krieg, W. J. S. *Brain Mechanisms in Diachrome.* Evanston, Ill.: Brain Books, 1955.

77. Lazarus, A. A. *Behavior Therapy and Beyond.* New York: McGraw-Hill, 1971.

78. Leibniz, G. W. *Philosophical Papers and Letters.* Dordrecht, Holland: R. Reidel Publishing Company, 1970.

79. Lenneberg, Eric H. *Biological Foundations of Language.* New York: John Wiley & Sons, 1967.

80. Lerner, I. M. *Heredity, Evolution and Society.* San Francisco: W. H. Freeman and Company, 1966.

81. Levine, M. *Psychiatry and Ethics.* New York: Braziller, 1972.

82. Lewes, G. H. *The Life of Goethe.* New York: Ungar, 1965.

83. Lilly, J. C. *The Center of the Cyclone.* New York: Julian Press, 1972.

84. London, P. *Modes and Morals of Psychotherapy.* New York: Holt, Rinehart and Winston, 1964.

85. Luria, A. R. *Human Brain and Psychological Processes.* New York: Harper & Row, 1966.

86. Lustig. B. *Therapeutic Method in Soviet Psychiatry.* Bronx, N.Y.: Fordham University Press, 1963.

87. Maris, R. W. *Social Process in Urban Suicide.* Homewood, Ill.: Dorsey Press, 1969.

88. Margolis, J. Z. *Psychotherapy and Morality.* New York: Random House Press, 1966.

89. Maslow, A. *Toward a Psychology of Being.* New York: Van Nostrand-Reinhold, 1968.

90. Maslow, A. *The Farther Reaches of Human Nature.* New York: Viking, 1971.

91. Meltzoff, J., and M. Kornreich. *Research in Psychotherapy.* New York: Atherton Press, Inc., 1970.

92. Milechnin, A. *Hypnosis.* Bristol: John Worght and Sons, 1967.

93. Miller, E. M. *Brain Capacity and Intelligence.* Australian Association of Psychology and Philosophy, 1926.

94. Milner, P. and S. Glickman. *Cognitive Processes and the Brain.* New York: Van Nostrand-Reinhold, 1967.

95. Moll, A. *Hypnosis.* New York: Julian Press, 1958.

96. Monod, J. *Chance and Necessity.* New York: Alfred A. Knopf, 1971.

97. Moore, J. H., Ed. *Ideas in Evolution and Behavior.* Garden City, New York: Natural History Press, 1970.

98. Mosteller, F., D. P. Moynihan, et al. *Re-Analysis of the Coleman Report.* Cambridge: Harvard University Press, July 1972.

99. Muzzey, D. S. *Spiritual Heroes.* New York: Unger, 1959.

100. Nobile, Philip. "What Is the New Impotence?" *Esquire,* October 1972.

101. Padover, S. *Thomas Jefferson and American Freedom.* New York: Van Nostrand, 1965.

102. Nowell-Smith, P. H. *Ethics.* Gretna, La.: Pelican, 1954.

103. Papez, J. W. *Comparative Neurology.* New York: Hafner, 1961.

104. Perls, Hefferline and Goodman. *Gestalt Therapy.* New York: Julian Press, 1969.

105. Phillips, E. L., and D. N. Wiener. *Short Term Psychotherapy.* New York: McGraw-Hill, 1966.

106. Pierce, J. S. *Crack in the Cosmic Egg.* New York: Julian Press, 1971.

107. Plato. *The Dialogues.* New York: Random House (various editions), 1939.

108. Postman, Louise. Unpublished research performed in

Massachusetts as reported to author by Dr. Postman.

109. Pound, E. *Confucian Analects.* London: P. Owen, 1956.

110. Powell, E. H. "Occupational Status and Suicide: Toward a Redefinition of Anomie." *American Sociology Review* 23: 131-139, 158.

111. Rachlin, H. *Introduction to Modern Behaviorism.* San Francisco: W. H. Freeman and Company, 1970.

112. Reich, Wilhelm. *An Introduction to Orgonomy.* New York: Noonday, 1970.

113. Reznikoff, M., and L. C. Toomey. *Evaluation of Changes Associated with Psychotherapy.* Springfield: Thomas, 1959.

114. Richter, D. *Aspects of Learning and Memory.* New York: Basic Books, Inc., 1966.

115. Rogow, A. A. *The Psychiatrists.* New York: Putnam, 1970.

116. Rosenhan, D. L. "On Being Sane in Insane Places." *Science* 19: 250-258, 1973.

117. Rosenthal, D. *Genetic Theory and Abnormal Behavior,* New York: McGraw-Hill, 1970.

118. Rubin, R. D., and C. M. Franks. *Advances in Behavior Therapy, 1968.* New York: Academic Press, 1969.

119. Russell, B. *The Analysis of Mind.* New York: Macmillan, 1921.

120. Russell, B. *Meaning and Truth.* London: Allen and Unwin, 1940.

121. Russell, B. *Philosophy of Leibniz.* London: Kimble and Bradford, 1937.

122. Russell, B. *Human Knowledge.* New York: American Book-Stafford Press, Inc., 1968.

123. Sanders, R., R. S. Smith, and B. S. Weinman. *Chronic Psychoses and Recovery.* San Francisco: Jossey-Bass, Inc., 1967.

124. Sargent, H. D., et al. *Prediction in Psychotherapeutic Research.* New York: International University Press, 1968.

125. Sarkisov, S. A. *The Structure of Functions of the Brain.* Bloomington, Ind.: Indiana University Press, 1966.

126. Scarff, M. "He and She: The Sex Hormones and Behavior." *The New York Times Magazine,* May 7, 1972, p. 30.

127. Schlesinger, B. *Higher Cerebral Function and Their Clinical Disorders.* New York: Grune and Stratton, 1962.

128. Schmidhoffer, Ernst. *Cerebral Training: An Application of Clinical Neurophysiology.* New York: Hafner, 1969.

129. Schofield, Wm. *Psychotherapy: The Purchase of Friendship*. New York: Prentice-Hall, 1964.

130. Seiden, R. H. "Campus Tragedy: A Study of Student Suicide." *Journal of Abnormal Psychology* 71(6):389-399, 1966.

131. Shaw, F. J., Ed. *Behavioristic Approaches to Counseling and Psychotherapy*. University of Alabama, 1961.

132. Shepard, M. *The Love Treatment*. New York City: Peter H. Wyden, Inc., 1971.

133. Shepard, M. and M. Lee. *Games Analysts Play*. New York: G. P. Putnam's Sons, 1970.

134. Shepard, M. and M. Lee. *Marathon 16*. New York: G. P. Putnam's Sons, 1969.

135. Shub, David. *Lenin*. New York: Mentor, 1950.

136. Singer, E. *Key Concepts in Psychotherapy*. New York: Random House, 1965.

137. Skinner, B. F. *Beyond Freedom and Dignity*. New York: Alfred A. Knopf, 1971.

138. Skinner, B. F. *The Behavior of Organisms: An Introduction to Behavior Theory*. New Haven, Conn.: Yale University Press, 1952.

139. Smith, C. U. M. *The Brain*, Chicago: University of Chicago Press, 1963.

140. Smythies, J. R. *Brain Mechanisms and Behavior*. New York: Academic, 1970.

141. Sorell, Walter. *The Duality of Vision*. Indianapolis: Bobbs-Merril, 1970.

142. Spencer, H. *Data of Ethics*. Street and Smith, 1902.

143. Spinoza, B. de. *Chief Works of Spinoza*. New York: Dover, 1961.

144. Stollak, G. E. *Psychotherapy Research*. Chicago: Rand McNally Psychology Series, 1966.

145. Stieper, D. R. and D. N. Wiener. *Dimensions of Psychotherapy*. Chicago: Aldine-Atherton, 1965.

146. Strupp, H. H., et al. *Patients View Their Psychotherapy*. Baltimore: Johns Hopkins University, 1969.

147. Strupp, H. H., and T. Bergin. "Some Empirical and Conceptual Bases for Coordinated Research in Psychotherapy." *International Journal of Psychiatry*. vol. 7, no. 2, February, 1969.

148. Stuart, R. D. *Trick or Treatment: How and When Psychotherapy Fails*. Champaign, Illinois: Research Press, 1970.

149. Stukat, K. G. *Suggestibility*. Stockholm: Almquist and Wiskell, 1958.

150. Szasz, T. S. *Pain and Pleasure*. New York: Basic Books, Inc., 1957.

151. Szasz, T. S. *The Ethics of Psychoanalysis*. New York: Basic Books, Inc., 1965.

152. Szasz, T. S. *Ideology and Insanity*. Garden City, New York: Anchor, 1970.

153. Szasz, T. S. *The Manufacture of Madness*. New York: Harper & Row, 1970.

154. Szasz, T. S. *The Myth of Mental Illness*. Hoeber-Harper, 1961.

155. Terman, L. M. *Scientists and Nonscientists in a Group of 800 Gifted Men*. American Psychological Association, 1954.

156. Tobias, P. U. *The Brain in Hominid Evolution*. New York: Columbia University Press, 1971.

157. U.S. Department of Health, Education and Welfare, Public Health Service, Current Editions:

Health, Education and Welfare Trends
Patients in Mental Institutions
Annual Statistical Report of Outpatient Psychiatric Services
Mental Health Statistics—Current Reports

158. U.S. Department of Health, Education and Welfare, Public Health Service, *Vital Statistics of the United States*, current issues and various supplements.

159. U.S. Department of Health, Education and Welfare, Public Health Service, *Suicide in the U.S., 1950-1964*, Series 20, No. 5, 1967.

160. Volgyesi, F. A. *Hypnosis of Men and Animals*. Baltimore: Williams & Wilkins, 1966.

161. Walker, N. *History of Psychotherapy*. London: Routledge and Kegan Paul, 1957.

162. Ward, Ingeborg. "Sexual Determinants of Behavior." *Science*. January, 1972.

163. Watson, J. B. *Behavior*. New York: Holt, Reinhart and Winston, various editions.

164. Watson, J. B. *Behaviorism*. Chicago: University of Chicago Press, 1958.

165. Weatherhead, L. D. *Psychology, Religion and Healing*. London: Hodder and Stoughton, 1963.

166. Wilhelm, R. *Confucius*. New York: Harcourt Brace, 1931.

167. Wittgenstein, L. *Tractactus Logico—Philosophicus*. London: Routledge and Kegan Paul, 1961.

168. Wittgenstein, L. *Philosophical Investigations*, 3rd ed. New York: Macmillan, 1969.

169. Wittgenstein, L. *A Lecture on Ethics*. In J. H. Gill's *Philosophy Today*, No. 1, New York: Macmillan, 1968.

170. Wolpe, J. *Behavior Therapy Practice*. New York: Pergamon, 1969.

171. Yates, A. J. *Behavior Therapy*. New York: John Wiley & Sons, 1969.

172. ———. *Relative Effectiveness of Psychotherapeutic Programs*, no. 492, Psychological Monographs, American Psychological Association, 1960.

173. ———. *Psychiatric Research Reports*, no. 6, American Psychiatric Association, October 1956.

174. ———. "Student Suicides." *British Medical Journal* 5122: 633, 1959.

175. Private, unpublished source.

176. Various references documenting the Soviet use of insane asylums to suppress dissent:

Newsweek, June 29, 1970, p. 47.
The Washington Post, August 2, 1970, p. B5.
The Washington Post, August 26, 1970, p. A20.
The Washington Post, September 22, 1970, p. A17.
The Washington Post, October 18, 1970, p. B2.
The Washington Post, April 3, 1971, p. A1.
The Washington Post, September 3, 1972, p. C1.
Medvedev, I. *A Question of Madness*. New York: Alfred A. Knopf, 1971.

177. Various sources documenting deleterious effects of "mind expanding drugs":

Maugh, T. H., II. "LSD and the Drug Culture: New Evidence of Hazard." *Science*, 23 March 1973, p. 1221.
Rafaelsen, O. J., et al. "Cannabis and Alcohol." *Science*, 2 March 1973, p. 920.
Casswell, S. and D. F. Marks. "Cannabis and Temporal Disintegration in Experienced and Naive Subjects." *Science*, 23 February 1973, p. 803.
Grilly, D. M. "Lack of Tolerance to Δ9-Tetrahydrocannabinol

in Chimpanzees." *Science,* 2 February 1973, p. 490.

Galanter, M. "Effects on Humans of Δ9-Tetrahydrocannabinol Administered by Smoking." *Science,* 26 May 1972, p. 934.

Renault, P. E., et al. "Marihuana: Standardized Smoke Administration and Dose Effect Curves on Heart Rate in Humans." *Science,* 29 October 1972, p. 523.

Abel, E. L. "Marihuana and Memory." *Science,* 10 September 1971, p. 1038.

Mikes F., and P. G. Waser, "Marihuana Components." *Science,* 11 June 1971, p. 1158.

Hollister, E. "Marihuana in Man." *Science,* 2 April 1971, p. 21.

Lemberger, L. et al. "Marihuana: Studies on Disposition and Metabolism of △9-Tetrahydrocannobinol in Man." *Science,* 18 December 1970, p. 1320.

Melgos, F. T. "Marihuana and Temporal Disintegration." *Science,* 29 May 1970, p. 1118.

Massett, L. "Marihuana and Behavior." *Science News,* 7 February 1970, p. 156.

Grinspoon, L. "Marihuana." *Scientific American,* December, 1969.

Weil, A. T., et al. "Clinical and Psychological Effects of Marihuana in Man." *Science,* 13 December 1968, p. 1234.

National Commission on Marihuana and Drug Abuse. *Marihuana: A Signal of Misunderstanding.* 2 vols. Washington: U.S. Government Printing Office, 1972.

Canadian Commission of Inquiry into the Non-medical Use of Drugs. *Cannabis.* Ottawa: Information Canada, 1972.

178. Various World Almanacs:

New York Times Almanac, 1972.

Information Please Almanac, 1972.

179. Selected References on Humanistic Psychology:

a. Waldman, R. D. *Humanistic Psychiatry.* New Brunswick, N. J.: Rutgers University Press, 1971.

b. Sutich, A. J. and M. A. Vich. *Readings in Humanistic Psychology.* New York: Free Press, 1969.

c. Perls, F. S. *In and Out of the Garbage Pail.* Lafayette, Calif.: Real People Press, 1969.

d. Perls, F. S., et al. *Gestalt Therapy.* New York: Julian Press, 1969.

e. Perls, F. S. *Ego, Hunger and Aggression, The Beginning of Gestalt Therapy,* New York: Random House, 1969.

f. Criswell, E., and S. Petersen. "The Whole-Soul Catalogue of Humanistic Psychology." *Psychology Today*, April, 1972.
g. Koch, S. "Can Psychology Be a Coherent Science?" *Psychology Today*, July, 1971.
h. Maslow, A. *The Farther Reaches of Human Nature*. New York: Viking, 1971.
i. Maslow, A. *Toward a Psychology of Being*. New York: Van Nostrand-Reinhold, 1968.
j. *Journal of Humanistic Psychology*, complete collection.
180. Various references in behavioral genetics:
a. Darlington, D. C. *The Evolution of Man and Society*. New York: Simon and Schuster, 1969.
b. Hirsch, J. *Behavior-Genetic Analysis*. New York: McGraw-Hill, 1967.
c. Manosevitz, M. *Behavioral Genetics*. New York: Appleton-Century-Crofts, 1969.
d. Gaito, J. *DNA Complex and Adaptive Behavior*. New York: Prentice-Hall, 1971.
e. Joffe, J. *Prenatal Determinants of Behavior*. New York: Pergamon, 1969.
f. Robinson, D. *Heredity and Achievement*. New York: Oxford University Press, 1971.
g. Thiessen, D. D. *Gene Organization and Behavior*. New York: Random House, 1972.
h. Parsons, P. *The Genetic Analysis of Behavior*. London: Methuen, 1967.
181. Selected references on the biological basis of language:
a. Chomsky, N. *Language and Mind*. New York: Harcourt, Brace, Jovanovich, 1972.
b. Chomsky, N. *Syntactic Structures*. The Hague: Mouton, 1968.
c. Cohen, M. S. R. *Language: Its Structure and Evolution*. Coral Gables, Florida: University of Miami, 1970.
d. McDonough, G. E. *The Origin of Man*. San Diego, 1953.
e. Revesz, G. *The Origins and Prehistory of Language*. Westport, Conn.: Greenswoot Press, 1970.
f. Wilson, R. A. *The Miraculous Birth of Language*. New York: New York Philosophies Library, 19.
g. Lenneberg, E. H. *Biological Foundations of Language*. New York: John Wiley & Sons, 1967.
182. Selected references on the psychology of genius:

a. Snow, C. P. *The Two Cultures and a Second Look.* New York: Mentor, 1964.
b. Kretschmer, E. *The Psychology of Men of Genius.* Washington: McGrath, 1970.
c. Lewandowski, H. *Genie und Eros,* 3 vols., Olten (Schweiz) Delphi-Verlag, 1950-52.
d. Schwartz, O. L. *General Types of Superior Men.* Boston: R. G. Badger, 1916.
e. Sorell, Walter. *The Duality of Vision.* New York: Bobbs-Merril, 1970.
f. Terman, L. M. *Scientists and Non-scientists in a Group of 800 Gifted Men.* American Psychological Association, 1954.
g. Wolfe, D. M. *The Image of Man in America,* 2nd ed. New York: Crowell, 1970.
h. Stern, A. *The Making of a Genius.* Miami Hurricane House, 1971.

183. Selected References on Psychotherapy, Placebos and Relevant Factors:

a. Kissel, P., and D. Barraucand. *Placebo et Effet Placebo en Médecine.* Paris: Masson, et cie. 1964.
b. Rosenthal, D., and J. D. Frank. "Psychotherapy and the Placebo Effect." *Psychological Bulletin,* vol. 53, no. 4, July 1956.
c. Gliedman, Litt. et al. "Reduction of Symptoms by Pharmacologically Inert Substances and by Short-term Psychotherapy." *A. M. A. Archives of Neurology and Psychiatry* 79: 343-351, March 1958.
d. Frank, J. D., et al. "Immediate and Long-term Symptomatic Course of Psychiatric Outpatients." *American Journal of Psychiatry,* vol. 120 no. 5, Nov. 1963.
e. Nash, E. H., et al. "Selected Effects of Inert Medication on Psychiatric Outpatients." *American Journal of Psychotherapy* XVIII (1):33-48, March, 1964.
f. Stone, A. R., et al. "The Role of Nonspecific Factors in Short-term Psychotherapy." *Australian Journal of Psychology* 18(3):210-217, 1966.
g. Hoehn-Saric, R., et al. "Systematic Preparation of Patients for Psychotherapy. I: Effects on Therapy Behavior and Outcome." *Journal of Psychiatric Research* 2:267-281, 1964.
h. Nash, E. H., et al. "Systematic Preparation of Patients for Short-term Psychotherapy. II: Relation to Characteristics of

Patient, Therapist and the Psychotherapeutic Process." *Journal of Nervous and Mental Disease*, vol. 140, no. 5, 1965.

i. Stone, A. R., et al. "An Intensive Five-Year Follow-Up Study of Treated Psychiatric Out-patients." *Journal of Nervous and Mental Disease*, vol. 133, no. 5, Nov. 1961.

j. Imber, S. D., et al. "A Ten-Year Follow-Up Study of Treated Psychiatric Outpatients." In S. Lesse *An Evaluation of the Results of Psychotherapies*. Springfield: Thomas, 1968.

k. Frank, J. D. "Therapeutic Factors in Psychotherapy." *American Journal of Psychotherapy* XXV:(3)350-361, July 1971.

l. Frank, J. D. "The Bewildering World of Psychotherapy." *Journal of Social Issues*, vol. 28, no. 4, 1972.

Index